AURELIA G. MACE.

"I will lift up mine eyes unto the hills from whence cometh my help."

AURELIA'S BOOK.

THE ALETHEIA.

THE ALETHEIA:

SPIRIT OF TRUTH.

A SERIES OF LETTERS IN WHICH THE PRINCIPLES
OF THE UNITED SOCIETY KNOWN AS SHAKERS
ARE SET FORTH AND ILLUSTRATED.

By AURELIA G. MACE.

———

*God is our Infinite Mother; She will hold us in her
arms of blessedness and beauty forever and ever.*
THEODORE PARKER.

———

SECOND EDITION.

———

FARMINGTON, MAINE:
PRESS OF THE KNOWLTON & McLEARY CO.
1907.

TO
"MY TEN," GEMS OF PRICELESS WORTH,
I AFFECTIONATELY DEDICATE THIS
BOOK.

AURELIA.

INTRODUCTION.

WITH the object in view that the Shakers may become better known, this book is offered to the public.

The first part comprises a series of letters that were published in *The Messenger*, a Bangor (Maine) paper, during the years 1883 and 1884. Then are inserted communications and short articles that have been published from time to time in the *Shaker Manifesto*.

It is presumed that by reading this book one can obtain a clear and correct idea of the Shakers' belief and manner of life, and of the rise and progress of the Societies.

We have been with you more than one hundred years, and still are not understood.

The mission of the Shaker is to live the pure life which Jesus lived and taught. Its meaning is to subdue and triumph over the animal nature in man, and to develop the spiritual nature. This is done by self-denial. The self-denial that the Prophet Daniel lived out, which made him the perfect man, greatly beloved, beautiful in form and feature, who could stand before the kings of the earth and confound them, and reveal what was hidden in the past and in the future.

As a Society, we, at Sabbathday Lake, have for many years been struggling for an existence, believing that we have something good and pure and beautiful to give unto the world when the world is able to receive it. " All cannot receive the saying. He that can receive it, let him receive it," said Jesus. The line is drawn and the life clearly defined. A man is a Shaker, or he is not. If he falls from the high standard, even in spirit, he ceases to be a Shaker until restored by the forgiving love of God.

In the service of the Society I have been at the Poland Spring House many times during the past twenty years, and have received great kindness and consideration from the people I have met within its walls. I have taken note of the grand and beautiful life fortune bestows upon her favored ones. I have had intercourse with the cultured, the refined and learned, and have great respect for the noble class of people I meet here from year to year. It has been with great joy that I have received many favors in behalf of my people, for which I am ever mindful and grateful.

Special thanks are due to the proprietors of the Poland Springs, also to Mrs. George Gregg, of Boston, Mass., and Mrs. J. Otis Swift, of Lewiston, Maine, for encouragement and assistance.

With a sincere desire that some good and no harm may be the result, this work is respectfully submitted.

A.

March, 1899.

CONTENTS.

ILLUSTRATIONS.

XIV   ILLUSTRATIONS.

SABBATHDAY LAKE, NEW GLOUCESTER, MAINE

SABBATHDAY LAKE.

UPON thy shores, O lovely lake,
  This calm, midsummer day,
I seem to hear a voice which tells
  Of ages passed away:

That, long before the birth of men,
  Through many waiting years,
You saw the forests rise, and heard
  The music of the Spheres;

And then the Indian came, from whence
  The mystery is sealed.
We question history, old and new,
  It has not been revealed.

But this we know, he trod these shores,
  His fields of maize here grew;
You saw the wigwam in the shade,
  You bore the bark canoe,

And here by simple nature taught,
  Ere science walked abroad,
In rolling waves and thunderings,
  He heard the voice of God.

Time fled, another race appeared,
  The former passed away,
And hunters gave the lake its name,—
  The name of Sabbathday.

2

For here they meet those sturdy men
    Of Puritanic race.
Each Sabbath found them here, this spot
    Became their trysting-place.

The years rolled by, the village grew,
    The mighty forests fell.
You saw the steeple rise afar,
    You heard the Sabbath bell.

You heard the whistle of the train
    Upon its iron rails.
The wilderness was all aglow
    Along the hills and dales.

O lovely lake, I walk thy shores,
    This calm midsummer day,
And muse on wonders thou hast seen
    In ages passed away.

LETTER I.

OUR HOME AT SABBATHDAY LAKE.

West Gloucester, January, 1883.

Editors of the Bangor Messenger:—

I thought you would like to know something of the Shaker Order, and therefore write you a letter from the heart of the village of this peculiar people. I am a Shaker myself, have been from childhood, and know whereof I speak.

Nothing could be more pleasing to us than to have all know of the hope that is in us, of the well-spring from which we drink, that has kept this community in gradual growth for more than one hundred years. It is favorable to any people to be liked best where they are best known. We find this to be the case with us.

Shaker Village, in West Gloucester, is very pleasantly situated on the eastern side of a small hill, surrounded on all sides by higher land. I can no better describe the place than in the words of an aged Shaker brother, Curtis Cramer, now visiting us, from the society in Cleveland, Ohio. He says: "Take a large wooden bowl and invert a smaller one inside of it, and you will get some idea of the situation."

The village is on the side of the smaller bowl, with a beautiful lake at its base, which is half a mile from the village on the east. We have a very fine view of the lake with the woodlands surrounding it at all seasons of the year; but in autumn the scenery is magnificent, abounding in many colors, with the passing clouds throwing their shadows upon them. The lake derived its name from a party of hunters, who, in the olden time, met on its shores every Sunday. Hence the Sabbath-day Lake.

Our government is a theocracy. We find a mother as well as a father in God, and are held together by bonds of pure love. Nothing else could do it. The life that Jesus lived is our example, and our order is founded upon the principles of that church that was organized at Jerusalem by his disciples. We have given up the private family life, and found in its place the great brotherhood and sisterhood which Jesus promised to those who would become his followers. All are loved and cared for. The rich and exalted come down and the poor are raised up, bringing all upon a Christian level.

Two miles north of us are the famous Poland Mineral Springs, with two large hotels accommodating many invalids, who come for the benefits derived from drinking the water, and thousands of others who come for the pleasure of this pleasant resort during the summer months. The hotels are first-class in every respect. Just one mile south are the Centennial Springs. We are surrounded by healing waters.

Thus you see that as was prophesied in days of old, the Sun of Righteousness has arisen upon us with healing in his wings, and there is a balm in Gilead by which the wounds of both body and soul can be healed. There is that Platonic love among us, which goes out to the suffering sons and daughters of men.

Have you a desire to know more of this peculiar people? "Ask and ye shall receive."

LETTER II.

THE DUALITY OF GOD—THE CHRIST SPIRIT.

February, 1883.

Editors of the Messenger :—

In the article that I recently contributed to your paper, I alluded to a subject which I wish to say more upon.

It may be that we, in looking abroad, see as much in the creeds of those outside which seems strange and unaccountable to us, as the casual observer finds among us that is hard for him to understand.

I would "walk with bare, hushed feet the ground" which I am about to enter. With due respect for the sincere belief of others, I must say that it seems strange to us that after all these years of increasing light, there should be any blind to the fact that we have a mother as truly as we have a father in God. "His eternal power and God-head" are understood by the things that are made, and all animal and vegetable life was created male and female. We have the authority of Moses that God said, "Let us make man in our image." Then they created a man and a woman. Is not this conclusive evidence of the duality of God?

How did Jesus become the Christ? Some who read this will say he was born the Christ, but we can not view it in that light. Nearly nineteen hundred years ago a man lived a very pure life and went about doing good, until the beautiful Spirit of Christ descended and abode upon him. He was not the first man that received the anointing power of Christ, neither was he the last. About four hundred years before Jesus was born, Socrates, by his self-denying life, received in a measure, the baptism of the Christ Spirit. Also Plato; so much so, that we can not think it sacrilegious to call him Plato the Christ.

These great men of old may have made mistakes; but the principles which they carried out in their lives, and taught to others, did not so far diverge from those afterwards promulgated by Jesus, as the lives of some who call themselves Christians in our day. Can a follower of Jesus the Christ go to war with his fellow-men?

I claim that there are those now living in our order, those "with whom my feet have trod the quiet aisles of prayer," who by a close walk with God have attained the Christ Spirit, and the same may be said of many who are not of this fold.

A few lines in regard to our situation here may be acceptable. One mile from our home, and just half-way between us and the Poland Mineral Springs, on the north, is another Shaker village very beautifully situated on the first and highest of the Rang Hills.

There are three hills that range side by side toward the north, each with a small lake on the west. The fathers and mothers of old gave them the name of the Rang Hills and the Rang Ponds, calling the name Rang instead of Range.

Poland Mineral Springs are on the middle Rang Hill. From the tower of the Poland Spring House, can be seen, with all the surrounding country, the Rang Hill on the north, the Rang Hill on the south, with the Shaker village thereon, and the three lakes to the west. In a clear day the White Mountains towards the northwest, and the cities of Lewiston and Auburn to the northeast are in plain view, and far to the southeast the ocean, until it is lost in the azure sky.

On pleasant afternoons in summer, we often enjoy delightful rides over these hills. At the hotels we have always been treated with great politeness. Hiram Ricker & Sons, proprietors of the two Poland Spring Houses, have ever shown the greatest kindness to us, as a people, for which they have our sincere thanks.

POLAND SPRING HOUSE.

LETTER III.

March, 1883.

Editors of the Messenger :—

Between our village and New Gloucester Upper Corner on the east, is a forest of tall, straight pine trees, the beautiful evergreens of our northern land. How often, in riding by them and walking in their shade, we have felt the force of that marvelous power that is able to change the scenery around us into poetry. It is the eyes that see, and the ears that hear with acuteness, that can find "tongues in trees, sermons in stones, books in the running brooks and good in everything" by which we are surrounded.

From the fertile soil of our domain, spring spontaneously the rock and white maple. The present season is so backward, and the snows are lying so deeply, that we have not yet commenced to rob them of their nectar. A few days more and they must yield to the sovereignty of man. Beautiful trees, standing in your pride and strength, you find in man your lord and master!

I propose to answer a question universally asked in regard to our community. It is a fact well known that we live the virgin life; and the question is: "What would become of the world if all should be Shakers?" I have heard it said that it is characteristic of the Yankees, that they answer one question by asking another; so I will answer this question by asking a number. What would become of the world if all should go to war and slay their fellow-men? What would become of the world if all that grows from the ground should be kept for seed to reproduce its like, and no portion of it saved for the higher use of sustaining life? What would become of the world if that great day of judgment should come "in the twinkling of an eye," according to the literal sense in which it is understood by many from a misinterpretation of the Scriptures?

It has been said that war and pestilence are necessary evils to check an over-abundant population. If this is so, it would be well if the Shakers were more numerous, that the check might come in a humane way, and those evils become exterminated.

All will admit that Jesus lived the highest life that could be lived by man; and he expressly declares: "All cannot receive this saying save they to whom it is given." "He that is able to receive it let him receive it." He afterwards said to those who had received the saying: "Ye are the light of the world;" and again, "Ye are not of the world," for to them had already come the end of the world, the Day of Judgment. Let those who cannot receive the saying become perfect in their generations. In so doing they will receive all the good that is to be found in the marriage relation.

Ann Lee was the founder of the Shaker community. She came to America from Manchester, England, in the year seventeen hundred seventy-four, accomplished her great work and died ten years from that time, at the age of forty-eight.

She possessed a powerful magnetism by which she seemed to control, easily, all within the sound of her voice. Thousands believed her words, and gave themselves, together with all their worldly goods, to support her cause. Bringing their property together, they organized these communities, which remain and flourish to this day.

We claim that she was inspired and directed by a power beyond that law of which Ingersoll speaks and writes, that she was the developing medium of mighty principles, eternal as the hills, that must yet undermine and destroy all false creeds. Already we see the writing upon the wall, and no Daniel is needed for its interpretation. The light of the present day is revealing to many those same principles, so clearly seen and set forth by our Mother, more than one hundred years ago.

One of these principles is, eternal progression in the life beyond. The travel of the soul from one degree of grace and glory to another throughout the endless ages of eternity.

She also received and transmitted to her followers that power which has held these communities together through the years that have passed, while those founded on other theories have failed.

We would have all who advocate the rights of women understand that our Mother gave unto her daughters, equal rights with their brothers in all the offices established for the government of the Shaker Order.

That Scripture is being fulfilled before our eyes: "The wolf also shall dwell with the lamb," etc. "And they shall beat their swords into ploughshares, and their spears into pruning-hooks," and they shall learn war no more.

HESTER ANN ADAMS.

Formerly of the Maine Ministry.

What shall I render to thee,
          My Father?
What shall I bring as a
Tribute of love to thee,
          My Mother?
A humble heart, a contrite spirit,
A virgin life, I bring unto thee.

                              H. A. A.

LETTER IV.

*W. D. HOWELLS—LAFAYETTE—MOTHER ANN'S
VOYAGE TO AMERICA.*

May, 1883.

Editors of the Messenger :—

Having been indulged with space in your columns a
number of times, I am encouraged to write again.
What most impels me is the desire that our principles
and standing may become better known to those outside.
We would speak to the people and earnestly solicit a
hearing; that those so inclined may investigate what has
hitherto been so little understood.

But few in comparison know of that germ which
started into growth contemporary with the glorious
Republic itself, that is yet to become a great tree,
giving shelter to many weary souls, and healing to the
nations.

We have been brought before the public in "The
Undiscovered Country," by W. D. Howells. To my
understanding he leaves the country undiscovered, or
the world in doubt of its existence. The work shows
that the Shakers felt sure of a future life of happiness,

but also a chance that they were mistaken. Of the child that had died, the outside man said: "If it knows anything." But the Shaker said: "We are sure that it knows." Friend Howells is very fair and correct in what he says about the angel life; but hardly gives credit to our people for the intelligence which belongs to them. In our ranks are found men with a collegiate education, and women learned and cultured.

Ann Lee, our Mother, had visions of Divine Beings from her childhood. She walked with God, revealed to her by the spirits of the just made perfect: "I saw two bright angels of God standing by the mast" were her words to the captain when the water was rushing into the ship, "through whom I received this promise: There shall not a hair of our heads perish. We shall all arrive safely in America." She then assisted with her own hands at the pumps. Shortly after this a large wave struck the ship with great violence, and the loose plank was instantly closed in its place.

This was viewed by all on board as a miraculous interposition of Divine Providence in their favor, and Mother Ann and her eight followers were treated with great respect and kindness during the remainder of the voyage. The captain was ever afterwards free to declare, that had it not been for these people, he would have been sunk in the sea and never reached America. They landed in New York the sixth day of August, 1774.

Lafayette, while he was in this country in the time of

the Revolutionary War, once visited Mother Ann and conversed with her, and witnessed the worship of her people, saw them moved by an occult power. He drew near to Abijah Wooster, a very gifted young man, and tried to take hold of his hand. Abijah said to him, " Do you love this power?" Lafayette made answer, " It is something that seems greatly to be desired."

These people held daily converse with their friends in spirit life many years before the spiritual manifestations commenced at Rochester, N. Y. It seemed as though bright beings from the throne of Eternal Majesty came down and ministered to them heavenly gifts; and the promised Millennium had commenced.

Thus the evidence is brought to our senses that we exist after death and that there is a God, the Great First Cause and Creator of all things. Not because the Bible tells us so, but from present revelations.

All things invented, made or created, must be originated by minds superior to the things thus brought into existence, so this great universe must have been formed by a Being far superior to itself. Is not this " Proof Palpable of Immortality"?

> " I am, O God, and surely Thou must be,
>   Thy light, Thy love, in their bright plenitude
>   Filled me with an immortal soul, to spring
>   Over the abyss of death, and bade it wear
>   The garments of eternal day, and wing
>   Its heavenly flight beyond this little sphere
>   Even to its source, to Thee its Author there ! ''

This is the faith which we have received and we are fettered by no creed, but as Friend Howells says, live the angel, virgin life, the life that Jesus lived. Or we are ever striving to come as near to that as possible.

A large dwelling-house is being built in our village, so business is unusually lively. To-day the granite blocks are moving fast into place, forming the basement; the three stories above to be of brick. The granite is taken from a quarry on our farm about a mile from the village.

These are fine May days; the farmers are putting the seed into the ground, the garden is planted and the roots set out, but we have yet to see the first dandelion blossom and buttercup of the Spring; trailing arbutus flowers are brought in and there are none more lovely or sweet, giving good cheer to all. The birds are busily repairing their little dwellings in the trees. To walk out into the beautiful day and drink in the blessings around us is joy unspeakable.

ELDER JOHN WHITELY.

*Bishop of the Societies in Massachusetts in which was laid the plot of the
" Undiscovered Country," by W. D. Howells.*

" I have feet, with God they 're walking,
　　For with gospel peace they 're shod ;
Most familiarly I 'm talking
　　As I take my walk with God.

" I have ears to hear the story
　　Men and angels love to tell ;
Eyes to see the rising glory
　　Which shall Zion's triumphs swell."

LETTER V.

June, 1883.

Editors of the Messenger:—

June is here in all her loveliness, the most beautiful season of the year.

On either side of the street which runs north and south, are to be seen lilac bushes in full bloom, both white and colored. In the row of shade trees extending the length of the village are the horse-chestnut, now in the height of their beauty. The large white trumpet-shaped blossoms pointing upward through the deep green foliage of the trees, are a sight one is never tired of beholding. On the top of the hill at the west is an orchard of young apple trees, now in full bloom. Vine-yards, gardens, orchards, and cultivated fields all around us in whatever direction we turn our eyes, and in our hearts that peace which passeth understanding. Surely the Utopia of Sir Thomas More is outdone.

When night hath drawn her sable curtains over our heads, we look away into the far heavens, and behold

3

mystery upon mystery. There are now plainly to be
seen six stars of the first magnitude looking down upon
us. Spica in the constellation Virgo, toward the south-
west; Altair in Aquila, to the east; Arcturus, Deneb,
Antares and Vega, all glowing with light from an inex-
haustible fountain. Let us go to them, in imagination,
and from them, behold the stars that will look down
upon us, as far from them as they are from our little
Earth. Let us go to the farthest star in the Nebula of
Orion, and we shall come to no end, neither can we
comprehend any beginning.

As it is in regard to space, so is it also in regard to
time. That man never lived who could search out the
existence of the Almighty, the beginning or the end of
time. Aristotle said: "It is evident there is neither
space, nor time, nor vacuum beyond the residence of the
gods in the highest heavens." And this to us is unfath-
omable.*

We have before our eyes, the Immensity of Space,
without beginning or end, and we also know of the great
æon of God, there is neither beginning nor ending. It
is enough for us to have the evidence that we shall exist,
individual beings, when that Angel, with one foot upon
the sea, and the other upon the land, declares: "There
shall be time no longer." And this will be but the

---

*Since the date of the publication of this letter scientific investiga-
tions have made known the elements of ether and the wonderful power
of the X-ray.

beginning, the mystery of God will be finished, because we shall but just then begin to comprehend the deep things of the Almighty.

It is a strange idea that any should believe for one moment that a God, with the attributes of love and justice in His organization, could create an immortal being, and then punish him eternally with dreadful sufferings for a few failures at the commencement of his existence. Jesus represented this God as a father, tender and merciful to His children, and we can see nothing in His teachings to justify any such belief.

Every sin has its penalty, and each individual must suffer according to the measure of his transgressions, either in this life or the next. The punishment is but for reformation, and when reformation is complete, the soul is restored to happiness and peace.

In looking over the world, I hardly think we could find a soul without one spark of goodness, and all goodness is of God. The germs of goodness will develop and grow, and the tares will finally be destroyed, and cast into the fire of truth.

How many great improvements have been made within the present century, and how many evils have been driven from the land! The scourge of slavery might be called the greatest, which cost so many precious lives and is so well remembered by those of us who have arrived at the meridian of life. Above all the turmoil and the confusion extant, we behold the good prevailing, and the evil being constantly undermined, the signs of the times gradually tending to the perfect day, the Jubilee, the Millennium.

"A Father's hand, a Mother's care,
Is ruling o'er the billows there."

Scattered abroad over this fair land are the pleasant community homes of the Shakers, of whom you yet know but little. They are not homes of servitude and sorrow, but they are homes of liberty, cheerfulness and peace, where brothers and sisters enjoy each other's society in purity and refinement, realizing all the blessings that accrue from lives strictly disciplined in the school of Christ. "Come and see," for we want you to know.

JOHN B. VANCE.

Formerly Bishop of the Societies in Maine.

I imagine that many of earth's heroes have had to go to school a long time in that other world to learn even the elementary lessons of how to live properly.

J. B. V.

"Peace, peace, ye wild winds
That shake the dark forest,
Be still ye fierce tempests
That rock the great sea.
Your strength is as weakness,
Compared with the power
Of those, who from bondage
Have set themselves free."

LETTER VI.

THE THREE CARDINAL PRINCIPLES—CONFESSION—
CELIBACY—COMMUNITY OF INTERESTS.

July, 1883.

Editors of the Messenger:—

Shall I write you a Sunday letter? Here in the still-
ness of the afternoon, sitting by my writing table, I recall
the events of the day.   At ten o'clock we went to church,
where many people had assembled to witness the worship of the Shakers.   It seems there were various causes
that drew them.   Some came merely for the recreation
of a Sunday ride, some for the amusement of seeing a
strange people, so different from " the rest of mankind,"
others from a sincere desire to find out our religious
belief.   This was held forth to them very plainly.

Would your readers like to know what was told the
people in our meeting to-day?   Then they will know
what they will have to do to become Christians.   (Ex-
cuse me, I look upon words Christians and Shakers as
synonymous.)

There are three principles unchangeable, that must be

met and digested at the beginning and strictly adhered
to in after life if we would be Shakers.

The questions of location, dress, diet, etc., are of
minor importance, still we aim at health and uniformity.

When you see how straight these three principles, of
which I am about to tell you, draw the line for our feet
to walk by, you may feel that it is a life hard to be attained, that, "This an hard saying; who can hear it?"

Can there be any greater crosses required under the
Shaker Covenant than were required by that Constitution which Lycurgus formed for the Spartans, by which
they rose to be such a brave people? Could our laws
bind us any more closely to a self-denying life than that
ideal government of Plato, which was never fully put
into practice?

The way is straight and narrow, and there are few that
find it. I tell you truly, I would rather be one of the
few than of the many. Buddha, long before Jesus,
pointed out "*The Path*," straight and narrow, devoid of
animal passions. His teachings were, in many ways,
similar to those of Jesus. "He that is compassionate
and observes the law is my disciple," said Buddha. "I
am not come to destroy the law, but to fulfill," said Jesus.

In defense of the Shaker Covenant, the Hon. John
Brethrett of Kentucky in his charge to a jury uses these
words: "And is it a matter of objection against any
man, that his motives are so pure and disinterested that
he desires to be released from earthly thralldom, that

SHAKER MEETING.

he may fix his thoughts and affections on his God? And after he has signed the Covenant he is released from earthly care.

"Much has been said against the Shaker Covenant. But, Sir, I repeat it, that individual who is prepared to sign the Church Covenant, stands in an enviable situation; who, devoted to God, is prepared to say of his property, 'Here it is, little or much, take it and leave me unmolested to commune with my God. Indeed I dedicate myself to what? Not a fanatical tenet; O no, to a subject far beyond, to the worship of Almighty God, the great Creator and Governor of the Universe. Under the influence of His love, I give my all; only let me worship according to my faith, and in a manner I believe acceptable to my God.'

"Now what is there objectionable in all this? I say again, the world can not produce a parallel to the situation such a man exhibits. Resigned to the will of Heaven, free from all feelings of earthly desires, and pursuing quietly the peaceful tenor of his way."

But you desire to know what these three principles are. I will tell you.

First—Confession. Every sin, secret or otherwise, must be confessed, one by one in the presence of a witness, whom we consider has attained a greater degree of the Spirit of Christ than ourselves. Now we have entered "*The Path*" hereafter there must be no more darkness in us. Our walk must be in the light.

Second—The Virgin Life. No longer to be controlled by animal passions. "Ye are harvested." "All can not receive this saying." But it must be received and lived out by the Shaker, the Christian.

Third—Community of Interests. The worldly goods which we possessed are no longer our own. We settle with our heirs, and pay all our debts, then, if there is anything left, we lay it "at the apostles' feet," for every man as he has need. This sacrifice is not accepted until the person has had time for due consideration. If after this, he withdraws from fellowship, the society is not obliged to restore to him what he thus freely gave; but there is generally a settlement made, mutually satisfactory.

From the doctrines of the confession of sin we find that the house built upon the sands of atonement of Christ must fall. Each must atone for himself, bringing his own deeds to judgment. From our dual God—Father and Mother—we find that the house built upon the sands of the Trinity must fall. There has been nothing created in the likeness of any such prototype as three male beings in one. Because we know that God is good, we find that the house built upon the sands of eternal punishment must fall. The door is open through the endless ages, for repentance and restoration.

These are truths according to the light that we have received, and we would not tear down and destroy the hopes of any, if we did not have something better, as we believe, to take their places.

ELIZA ANN TAYLOR.

Of the Central Ministry, Mt. Lebanon, N. Y.

"I will bless thee, O Zion," saith the Lord.
 "I will bring precious gifts to thee;
My word shall be written, my law shall be kept,
 And my house be a refuge free.
 My temple upbuilded shall be,
The corner-stone now I have laid,
 And the indwellers there
 On their foreheads shall bear
My name graved in letters of gold."

" Let, then, O God ! thy servants dare
Thy truth in all its power to tell,
Unmask the priestly thieves, and tear
The Bible from the grasp of hell ! ''

This is my Sunday letter, written in the silence of the afternoon. I submit it to you, feeling that it is lawful to do good on the Sabbath day.

The flowers are blooming, the birds are singing, and all is delightful. This rest was provided for us by a loving Father and a tender Mother.

LETTER VII.

THE ATONEMENT—THE GOD OF MOSES—THE GOD OF JESUS.

August, 1883.

Editors of the Messenger:—

The days of the last month of summer are fast slipping away. The browning fields and drooping limbs of the fruit-laden trees remind us that the harvest is near. Even now the birds are beginning to sing of their southward journey.

The large garden to the west of our village is producing more than its usual amount of seeds, fruits and vegetables. Potatoes are very nice, an abundant crop coming in, owing to the long war with their fell destroyers, the little emigrants in striped cloaks, which ended seemingly by their annihilation.

All the people are busily engaged in their various occupations. Thus by the sweat of the brow are we earning the bread that is to sustain us through the coming winter.

"The gods help those who help themselves," and even as the hand of help came to John Bunyan's pilgrim when he was in trouble, so are blessings being constantly strewn in our pathway, surrounded as we are at all times by the good, the pure, and the beautiful.

None can enjoy the beautiful, even in material things, like the virgin spirit; none can see God but the pure in heart, and in these lovely days which are so sweetly passing by, we

> " Salute you ; earth and air and sea and sky,
> And the imperial sun that scatters down
> His sovereign splendors upon grove and town ! "

In my last letter to you I spoke of the house founded upon the sands of the atonement of Christ, maintaining that, from the light in which we view the subject, it must fall. How can it be otherwise if it is a false theory? If it is the truth, God is unjust.

A God angry with a world of people that he himself had created, not for any sins of their own, but because their first father and mother committed one sin, and he could never become reconciled to any of them unless another God should be willing to be born into the world, grow to manhood and suffer death at the hands of these same people! Take into consideration also that this angry God had before made a special law for them, "Thou shalt not kill." How could a father coolly propose for his children to break the laws that he had given them, and then punish them eternally for doing so?

We do not believe that Jesus taught any such doctrine, and we also know that the God of Love that he represented was a being very different from the God revealed to the people by Moses. The life that Jesus lived was far in advance of that degree of civilization that his brethren, the Jews, had attained, and they cruelly put him to death, he in his dying moments declaring, "They know not what they do."

He said to his followers, "I am the Resurrection and the Life," showing plainly that if we would become one with him, we must follow his example in all things, living the life that he lived.

He looked into the future and saw that light and knowledge would increase, and that his followers would do even greater works than he had done.

There are many who believe that Jesus will some day come in the literal clouds, and the bodies of the dead will arise from their graves. That day will never dawn.

> "He cometh not a king to reign,
> The world's long hope is dim ;
> The weary centuries watch in vain
> The clouds of heaven for him."

But the spirit of Christ is always near, if we will but believe and obey. Let us, therefore, open our hearts to receive that love that will save us from committing sin, the lovely Christ Spirit, sent to us by our Heavenly Father and Mother—God.

> "At morn I prayed, I fain would see
> How Three are One and One is Three ;
> Read the dark riddle unto me."

ELDRESS DOROTHY ANN DURGIN.

East Canterbury, N. H.

To the Surest and the Purest I would give my life away.

D. A. D.

LETTER VIII.

NEW CENTER DWELLING—SCHOOL—NATHAN MER-
RILL AND THE FOUNDERS OF THE SOCIETY—
ELDER OTIS SAWYER.

November, 1883.

Editors of the Messenger:—

Since writing you last a number of months have rolled
their course. Business has been very active in our community, but we are now thinking of settling down to pass
the winter in our cosy apartments. Thanksgiving is at
hand. The sun is nearing its southern terminus, bringing Christmas with all its pleasant associations.

The new house, which was not to be seen one year ago
at this time, stands as a beautiful monument in our village. The garden-house, where the seeds are dried and
the garden tools stored, has been repaired the past summer. It looms up like a splendid cottage on the western
hill. The workmen have left, from the master-builders
down to the hod-carriers, excepting two carpenters.

The long term of school has commenced, to continue
until March. Each forenoon and afternoon, at the regular hours, we hear the little bell, calling the youth and

children together in the school-house, which is nicely
fitted up, north of the village, west side of the street.
Mulberry trees are set around the building, which will in
future days become a beautiful grove.

In passing the school-house door, we hear the happy
voices of little boys and girls in recitations or singing,
also the music of the pencil upon the slate and the
crayon upon the blackboard.

We are often invited to the school exhibitions, which
are very interesting. Then the little students vie with
each other to show the amount of diligence with which
they have studied; striving with hard questions upon
the blackboard, speaking dialogues, poetry, and even
delivering orations, generally ending with music. Words
of encouragement and good cheer, and often small pres-
ents, are then given to our dear little ones by their
guardians and friends.

Our present teachers have been brought up from
children and educated in this community. The school
stands upon an even basis with the other schools in New
Gloucester, and is under the supervision of the Superin-
tending School Committee of the town. Children outside of the Society who live near attend, and their parents seem to be well pleased with the progress they
make.

Just one hundred years ago the fourteenth day of this
month, the first inhabitant of this place was converted to
Shakerism. His name was Nathan Merrill. Within a

fortnight of that time, nearly all the families around came into this sacred union. In many cases a man's foes became those of his own household, for a man was set at variance against his father, and the daughter against her mother, and the daughter-in-law against the mother-in-law.

These were exciting days, and a goodly number from each family came into the joint relation. They could not close their ears to the voice of the Spirit of Christ, which was sounding in trumpet tones, "He that loveth father or mother more than me is not worthy of me, and he that loveth a son or daughter more than me is not worthy of me. And he that taketh not his cross and followeth after me, is not worthy of me."

These good fathers and mothers have long since passed on to those lovely mansions, made without hands, eternal in the heavens. Many of them lived to extreme old age. In early youth I was conversant with about fifty of them, and had them for my instructors. They had brought their lives under such strict discipline that no trial, however severe, could disturb the serenity of their spirits. I have seen them grieved but never ruffled.

Last evening I visited a library containing a copy of each book published by this Order since it was founded. It consists of one hundred and seventy-five volumes, with their revised editions.

These books have been collected and numbered, and the library set in order for the reception of other books that may be published by the untiring efforts of Elder Otis Sawyer. Future generations will look upon his works and call him blessed. In the way that Solomon built the Temple and that God made the world, so has he built the house that hath been reared in the midst of our village the past season. He said, "Let it be done," and it was done.

The storms of winter are approaching. Their harbingers have already been here, following a long and beautiful Indian summer, which, we trust, has been enjoyed by all.

MEETING-HOUSE AND CENTER DWELLING, SABBATHDAY LAKE, MAINE.

LETTER IX.

ORIGIN OF THE SHAKERS.

January, 1884.

Editors of the Messenger:—

To-day I find myself seeking out the beginning of Shakerism. The first thought draws me to a company of French prophets who went into England in the year seventeen hundred and six. They taught a high and pure religion, preparatory to a greater work that was to follow.

Those French prophets extended their warnings over the greater part of Europe. The few who went into England drew many into their ranks. They formed no regular societies until about the year seventeen hundred and forty-seven, when a small society was organized in the neighborhood of Manchester, under the leadership of James and Jane Wardley. They were very powerful ministers, and taught the confession of sin and purity of life.

In their meetings the people had wonderful manifestations of divine power, swiftly passing and repassing each other like clouds agitated with a mighty wind. From

4

these exercises they received the appellation of Shakers,
a very appropriate name, for the Lord hath said, "All
the men that are on the face of the earth shall shake at
my presence," etc.

When this little society was organized, Ann Lee, our
Mother, was eleven years of age, but did not unite with
these people until she was twenty-two.   She had been a
very peculiar child from infancy, serious and thoughtful,
not addicted to play like other children.   She often told
of having visions of supernatural things.   Her mother
was a good woman, able to instruct and guide her, but
she died when Ann was quite young, and left her with
no one to depend upon for help.   She was early married
to Abraham Stanley and had four children; but they all
died in infancy except one little girl, who attained the
age of six years.

In her married life she found nothing but condemna-
tion and sorrow, although her husband was very kind
and attentive to her.   She felt a yearning for a higher
life, and the burden of sin and the depravity of human
nature lay heavily upon her.   She found some releasement by uniting with James and Jane Wardley, strictly
adhering to their counsel and living up to the light of
their society.

The religious exercises of this little band stirred up
the opposition of the people around them, and they were
severely persecuted and often imprisoned, our Mother
receiving her share with the rest.

About this time Oliver Goldsmith was writing "The Vicar of Wakefield." In order to become acquainted with the condition of society in England at this period I refer the reader to that book. Those who excited prejudices by differing from others in sentiment or action, could expect but little justice and were often unmercifully abused.

It was in the summer of seventeen hundred and seventy that our Mother was imprisoned in Manchester, being falsely accused by her enemies of breaking the Sabbath. After a scene of deep tribulation of soul, when her way was seemingly hedged up on every side, and she cried mightily to God for deliverance, the rays of Divine Light suddenly broke in upon her spirit and the Heavens of Glory were spread before her in open vision. She saw the spirit of Jesus, and he spoke to her words of love and comfort, gave her a mission, assuring her of divine protection in its fulfillment, and revealed to her those principles upon which this Order has been founded, sacred, eternal and true.

When she was released from prison and returned to the society, her Elders, James and Jane Wardley, immediately saw that she had received light superior to theirs, and they and their people willingly acknowledged her as their leader. From this time onward she was called "Mother" by her faithful followers. It has been said, that, when under the power of the Holy Spirit, her countenance shone with the glory of God, and her form and actions appeared divinely beautiful and very angelic. The power and influence of her spirit, at such times, was great beyond description; and no one was able to gainsay or resist the authority by which she spoke.

I submit this letter to you, trusting that the message may be received, and with the prayer that the day may be hastened when "The knowledge of the Lord shall cover the earth as the waters cover the sea."

MARY ANN GILLESPIE.

Formerly of the Maine Ministry.

Let my name be recorded
  In the book the angels keep,
Where each act is rewarded
  And the seed I have sown I shall reap.
Then when the Angel Reaper cometh,
  And the harvest time shall be,
I shall find in my Father's house,
  There 's a mansion reserved for me.

                              M. A. G.

LETTER X.

MOTHER ANN'S PERSECUTIONS IN ENGLAND.

Editors of the Messenger:—

By your kindness, I have, transiently, been allowed space in your columns. Judging the future by the past I am encouraged to look for a continuation of the same. Many erroneous opinions are extant in regard to the Shakers, and it is but fair that their principles should become better known. Many who are uninformed are writing about them, and it is but just that the Shakers themselves should have a hearing. As I said in a former letter, we find ourselves to be best liked where we are best known, and some of your readers may desire to become better acquainted with a community that has prospered and gradually grown for more than one hundred years.

Many we behold who, for a closer walk with God, have been willing to forsake father, mother, wife and children, houses and lands, and their former lives, and have in return, even now, in these community homes, received an hundred fold of fathers and mothers,

brothers and sisters, houses and lands, and all the song
of their souls is:

> " Nearer, my God, to Thee, nearer to Thee;
>   E'en though it be a cross that raiseth me."

If one had always been blind and had never seen a
sunbeam, is there power in words to describe it so that
he could know of its beauty? If one had always been
deaf and had never heard the song of a bird, is there a
language by which it could be brought perfectly to his
understanding? Even so words fail of describing the
joys of the redeemed spirit.

> " Alone, O love ineffable,
>   Thy saving name is given.
>   To turn aside from thee is hell,
>   To walk with thee is heaven.
>
> " Thy litanies, sweet offices
>   Of love and gratitude;
>   Thy sacramental liturgies,
>   The joy of doing good."

In my last letter, I wrote you of the origin of the Shakers; that the first society was established in the year
seventeen hundred and forty-seven, and that our Mother,
Ann Lee, became its leader in the year seventeen hundred and seventy.

Her mission, calling people as it did, away from the
selfish private family life, into a great brotherhood and
sisterhood, and striking a deadly blow against those
indulgences which the carnally minded so much desire,

stirred up the opposition of many, and caused her to have relentless enemies.

Three attempts were made to take her life while she remained in England. Once she was locked in a prison, and kept, as her enemies thought, without food for fourteen days, with the intention of starving her. One of her followers, James Whittaker, whom we now call Father James, then a youth, went each night after the first and put the stem of a pipe through the key-hole of the door, and into the bowl of the pipe poured wine and milk, by which our Mother received nourishment that sustained her. It was with astonishment that her enemies saw her walk off with so much strength when they unlocked the door at the end of the fourteen days, expecting to find her dead.

At another time they accused her of blasphemy, and caused her to have a trial before four ministers of the Established Church, hoping that they would condemn her to have her tongue bored through with a hot iron. I am aware that this is dreadful to speak of in these days, but great cruelty prevailed at that time.

The ministers requested to hear her speak, and she spoke with such power that they dismissed her at once, and advised her accusers to let her alone.

This enraged them to such a degree that they determined to take the power of judgment into their own hands. They agreed to stone her for blasphemy, and led her into a valley. Some of her people followed and kept near her. Then her accusers took their places upon the hill opposite and commenced to throw stones, but missed their aim in every instance except one. One of the brethren was slightly injured. In a short time those men began to quarrel with each other and dispersed, leaving our Mother and her people to return in peace to their homes. In relating these circumstances to some of the believers she said: "While they were throwing their stones I felt myself surrounded with the presence of God, and my soul was filled with love. I knew they could not kill me, because my work was not done; therefore I felt joyful and comfortable, while my enemies felt distress and confusion."

Those were days when persecution walked rampant; when life was often taken in punishment for the expression of a religious opinion. But at that same time a home was being prepared in the wilderness of America, where freedom of thought could be tolerated, and "To the woman were given two wings of a great eagle, that she might fly into the wilderness, into her place."

ELDER WILLIAM DUMONT.

Sabbathday Lake, Maine.

" Who will walk in the midst of the flame
When the gospel fire is burning?
Who will endure to be made wholly pure
Without one shadow of turning?"

LETTER XI.

ROYAL'S RIVER—NOBLE PIONEERS OF THE TOWN—FIRST SHAKER MEETING IN NEW GLOUCESTER—ELDER ELISHA POTE—DEATH OF ELDER OTIS SAWYER—VISION OF MOTHER ANN.

May, 1884.

Editors of the Messenger:—

This morning the mist is rising from the water-courses and encircling the distant hills. Northeast of our village we can trace Royal's river through the "Woods of Pine," by the billow of mist which hangs over it, as it finds its way to the sea by a zigzag course.

> "The winding way the serpent takes,
>   The mystic river took,"

as in all the years that are past it has borne the overflow of Sabbathday Lake along through the green fields and meadows, around the hills and over the pasture lands, until it reaches the ocean at Yarmouth, eighteen miles from this place.

Up this river were poled on rafts the families and goods of our forefathers in the fall of the year seventeen hundred and forty-two, they having come by vessel from

ELDER OTIS SAWYER.

Formerly Bishop of the Societies in Maine.

"Like unto the grandeur of the eastern clouds when the sun is rising, so is the redeemed spirit."

Gloucester, Mass. The first settlement was then made upon the sunny slopes of those hills.

Until the time of this intrusion, the winding stream had been hurrying on, "unvexed by the wheels of industry," since that far-distant day when it was first called into being by the "Heart of Heaven."

> " Come forth, O Water of Serpents !
>   In sinuous, gliding grace
> Went forth the queenly river
>   Unto her chosen place.
> Then called he the youngest, the fairest,
>   Step softly, Water of Birds !
> And the silver-footed brook stole out,
>   Singing songs that had no words ! "

The French and Indian war broke up this settlement for a time. Their log-houses were destroyed and sawmill burned by the savages, and the people fled back to their old homes. They returned in the spring of seventeen hundred and fifty-four and built a fort or blockhouse, in which they lived six years, never going out unarmed.

The year seventeen hundred and sixty brought peace to the settlement. The old homes were soon restored, and the wilderness was made to blossom as the rose.

The names of men of stern integrity adorn the escutcheons of this town.

William Widgery was one of the pioneers, the man who was obliged by his charter to refuse Marshal Ney a passage to America in his vessel, upon the downfall of Napoleon.

Isaac Parsons, represented as the man with a stern look, built the first frame-house, which is still standing; and O how sacredly was the Sabbath observed in that house! His descendants are among the most respectable people living around us.

The Rev. Samuel Foxcroft was the Puritan minister, who for many years dispensed the word of God to a united people, required by law to attend to his teachings. When he laid down his charge in the year seventeen hundred and ninety-three it was with sorrow he saw his flock scattered, freedom of conscience leading each man his own way.

The first Shakers came to New Gloucester in November, seventeen hundred and eighty-three, and held meetings in the western part of the town. Their first meeting was held in the house of Gowen Wilson, Sr., which was situated in the field just south of our large garden, on the west side of the road. Elisha Pote, a young man from Gorham, Maine, took the lead in speaking. He had lately become a convert to the Shaker faith. His reasonings were clear and convincing, and his voice mild and persuasive.

Many believed the new doctrine, and the Shakers have occupied this ground from that day until the present time.

The society was organized on the nineteenth of April,

seventeen hundred and ninety-four. The society at
Alfred, Maine, had been organized a short time previous,
and another society in the town of Gorham soon after.

Elisha Pote afterwards became the spiritual leader of
the three Maine societies, and occupied that place many
years. He died at a great age, widely known and
respected by all.

His second successor was our well-beloved Elder Otis
Sawyer, who in the month of March, the present year,
went over to dwell in the Paradise of God, the "House
not made with hands, eternal in the heavens." Like a
beautiful cloud he moved from our sight, but the Comforter cometh. Upon the wings of the morning are
wafted these words to the sorrowing ones, "Peace I
leave with you, my peace I give unto you: not as the
world giveth, give I unto you," "and lo, I am with you
alway, even unto the end."

Why should we mourn when he is with us nearer than
before, when he is leading us in green pastures, and
beside the still waters? His pure and refined spirit has
become one with Christ, even as Christ is one with the
Heavenly and Eternal Father and Mother.

I will here add an item further in regard to that ocean
voyage of Ann Lee and her people. As I wrote you in
a former letter, the ship which brought them came very
near sinking in mid-ocean with all on board, and was
saved by a miracle. At that time the people of America
were commencing the struggle for independence. The

Angel of the Lord was seen by our Mother, passing on
in advance of the ship, singing with a mighty voice:

" From the Heaven of Heavens
   O'er sea and land I fly,
   Crying sweet, sweet liberty !
   Peace, peace upon earth,
   The hand of the Lord
   Has freed America.
   O bless this blessed day,
   Your freedom, freedom claim ;
   And prepare ye, all people,
   Salvation to gain."

IN THE WOODS OF PINE.

BEAUTIFUL trees of the primitive forests,
    Oft in your shades I'm delightfully led,
Culling the wild flowers, resting in green bowers,
    Where to my feet a rich carpet is spread.

Music of warblers free everywhere greets me,
    Blending in harmony's unwritten song;
Lo, from the depths profound, chanting a merry round,
    Onward the ocean-bound brook glides along.

Wonderful trees with your branches extending,
    Casting your shadows and shedding your dew,
Moved by the breezes, dependently bending,
    Gratefully clouds pass their shadows o'er you.

Mighty in strength, wealth, and pride in the nation,
    Waving in grandeur o'er mountain and plain,
If ye could speak, 'twould be, " Check the strong axe-man,
    Save and protect us, ye powers of Maine."

Thus the great Pine Tree State may by an effort
    Rescue the forests by which she is blest,
Finding in recompense treasures of excellence,
    Richer by far than the minds of the West.

Beautiful trees of the primitive forest,
    O how delightful to walk in your shade,
Culling the wild flowers, resting in green bowers,
    Where underfoot a rich carpet is laid!

ELDER ABRAHAM PERKINS.

[Age, 90 years.]

Formerly Bishop of the Societies in New Hampshire and Maine.

O beauteous resurrection morn!
My spirit unto thee is born;
    Thy elements I love.
Thy air I breathe, in thee I live,
The substance lost I now retrieve,
    Which opens heaven above,
    The world of light above.

A. P.

LETTER XII.

PROTESTATION I.

August, 1884.

Editor of The Increasing Light:—

Before me is one of your papers containing an article in regard to our people. The writer says that he strained his understanding long and earnestly to get clear on a certain point, and that he failed of satisfactorily finding out, when he attended our meeting on the Sabbath of the twenty-second of July. If he will lend us his attention a few moments we will enlighten him, but will first say that we notice several mistakes in his communication to which we greatly demur; and as we desire that our principles should become better known to those outside, it may be well to give your readers the other side of the story.

I attended the meeting of which he writes, but did not hear the gloomy things he tells about. "But this we confess unto you that after the way which they call heresy, so worship we the God of our fathers," believing in the inspired word. From my standpoint it was the worship of God in the beauty of holiness. Our reverend Elder stood before us, his silvery locks and goodness of heart entitling him to our love and respect, while he nobly held forth the word from a soul overflowing with love to God and humanity. "Thou shalt rise up before the hoary head, and honor the face of the old man and fear thy God; I am the Lord."

We do not believe in the Trinity. To us God is Father and Mother and has been from the beginning. In this we are sustained both by the Scriptures and reason. Jesus was an inspired man, Ann Lee was an inspired woman. Christ is the Anointing Power that all may receive. Inasmuch as Jesus became the Christ and as Ann Lee became the Christ, so may all be in possession of the same spirit to that degree which they make themselves worthy by good works.

We know that all can not be Shakers, and we have great respect for those parents who bring up their children "in the nurture and admonition of the Lord." We have no sympathy with the unfruitful works of darkness. We claim that the generative life is not the highest life. The example that Jesus set we strive to follow.

The celebrated veteran, Frederick Douglass, attended the meeting in question. He was staying at Poland Mineral Springs for his health, and gave us the pleasure of seeing him in the audience. This circumstance tended to carry our feelings back to those turbulent days through which our country passed and triumphed.

ELDER JOSHUA BUSSELL.

Alfred, Maine.

" Deep the river of life that 's flowing,
  Gently gliding serene and grand ;
Oh, the beauty of its crystal waters !
  Laving the shores of the promised land.
Sailing along on its peaceful bosom
  Are kindred souls, a happy band,
Filled with songs of joy and rejoicing
  As they near the promised land."

As we would lightly pass over the ridicule of the thoughtless so would we, like Phocion of old, scorn the applause of the giddy multitude; but we love goodness wherever it is found, and we love our Shaker brothers. They are worthy of our confidence and trust.

LETTER XIII.

PROTESTATION II.

August, 1884.

Editor of the People's News:—

In your paper of Saturday was a letter entitled "Among the Believers," and the thought struck me that you might give a place in your columns to a letter from one of the Believers.

In view of Sabbathday Lake, in view of the green slopes and in the shade of the round-topped apple trees, I am writing to you this sultry August day.

Yesterday was Sunday, and the "Little Church" was crowded. Many came from Poland Springs, two miles distant on the north. Auburn, Lewiston and Portland were also represented in the audience. All here to witness the worship of this peculiar people. Why peculiar? Because they have dared to differ from others. In looking round upon the people who filled our church, we could not help observing how many there were who saw us only in the light in which we were viewed by the lady whose letter appeared in your Saturday's paper. But there was a class there who saw things differently—who saw nobility and dignity in the Shaker brothers, who saw loveliness and beauty in the Shaker sisters' dress, which was not, my friend, "selected with a view to its ugliness;" that is a mistake, but with a view to utility and comfort. "Your tastes are perverted," said our good Elder Frederick Evans to one who failed to see beauty in the Shaker sisters' dress. "Bad diet has done it, or you have been wrongly educated."

Communications are often published in the secular papers in regard to the Shakers, written by those who understand but little of our principles or manner of life, in which we find wide deviations from the truth, and we desire a hearing. We have been with you one hundred years, and yet are in a great measure unknown to you.

The writer says that the Shaker brothers are honest. All that they sell proves to be just what they represent, and with the next breath, that the rhythm of their motions indicates "We are nothing, less than nothing. We are dreams." An honest man nothing but a dream! To me the rhythm of their motions means, "We are the noblest work of God!"

Now let us inform you, who see so little to admire in the pure life the Shakers lead, that we often see as much in your lives, in your beliefs and in your manner of dress that seems strange and unaccountable to us, as you can possibly see in ours that seems strange and unaccount-

able to you.   But we will wait for the future to weigh
all things, knowing that the truth will finally prevail.

> " God's ways seem dark, yet soon or late
>   They touch the shining hills of day ;
>   The evil cannot brook delay,
>   The good can well afford to wait ;
>   Give ermined knaves their hour of crime,
>   Ye have the future, grand and great,
>   The safe appeal of truth to time."

Sarah Fletcher.

Prudie Stickney.   Mamie Curtis.   "Aurelia."   Amanda Stickney.

Sirena Douglass.   Ada Cummings.   Lizzie Haskell.

SISTERS OF THE SABBATHDAY LAKE COMMUNITY.

FATHERS AND MOTHERS, AN HUNDRED FOLD GREETING.

[From the *Manifesto*.]

New Gloucester, April, 1884.

You whose spirits are replete with that perfect love which casteth out fear, in you is found that charity which never faileth, binding up the broken-hearted, strengthening the weak, and comforting the afflicted. In you is found that power which healeth the sick of sin, casteth out the spirits of evil, and giveth sight to those who are blinded to the true light and life.

By giving up all you have received all. For every sacrifice that you have made of selfish pleasures, an hundred fold of spiritual blessings has filled your cup to overflowing, and the pathway in which you walk is leading you nearer to the fountain of all good, nearer and nearer to God.

A few short years here in which to teach your disciples and followers to do as you have done, to live as you have lived, and then the real home in the Heaven of · Glory is opened unto you.

" They are slipping away, these sweet, swift years,
   Like a leaf on the current cast ;
   With never a break in their rapid flow,
   We watch them as one by one they go
      Into the beautiful past."

And one by one you go, beloved, into the beautiful future, into the home of the redeemed, a home that you have made your own by a travel of soul away, far away from sordid passions; redeemed from all that is not of God.

Like the lake in midsummer, when the air is still, so is the redeemed spirit. Like unto the tree clothed with the blossoms of spring, and like unto the tree laden with the ripe fruits of autumn, so is the redeemed spirit. Like unto the grandeur of the eastern clouds when the sun is rising, so is the redeemed spirit.

In the school of Christ you have been disciplined, by the fire in Zion you have been tried, until like the gold of Ophir you are purified; and now saith the Spirit, "Ye shall walk with me in white, for ye are worthy."

From this high estate, let your blessings descend like the dew of Hermon into the hearts of your faithful children. Let your mantles rest upon those who follow in your footsteps, and you shall be more than satisfied when the books are opened, and your eyes behold the record of those whom you have led along in the Highway of Holiness.

TRUSTEES' OFFICE, SABBATHDAY LAKE, MAINE.

THE CHRIST OF THE AGES.

CREEDS—BAPTISM—THE EUCHARIST—EQUALITY OF THE SEXES—THE BIBLE—THE ARTS AND SCIENCES.

[From the *Manifesto.*]

January 15, 1896.

" Ring out the darkness of the land,
Ring in the Christ that is to be."

In the January *Humanitarian* is a communication by Paul Tyner, entitled, "The Christ Ideal in Shakerism." He says that Mother Ann Lee believed that the spirit of Jesus came to her when she was in prison in Manchester, England. No doubt it was Jesus, the Christ, for from that time she was clothed with the Christ as with a garment.

In the prison, more than one hundred and twenty-five years ago, principles were revealed unto her which the development of the sciences have been unable to overthrow, principles that will stand to the end of time.

The revelation which she received was a harvest from the generative life. Also that the mission of Jesus upon the earth was to teach a higher life to those who were able to receive the doctrine.

When she returned to her people from the prison she took up the work where Jesus had left it, and her followers were not of the world, even as the followers of Jesus, in his day, were not of the world.

In the Order or the Community which she founded, she was second to Jesus. Jesus was the first to teach the higher life, Ann Lee was the second. Both were inspired by "The Christ." Our Mother being second to Jesus in the Shaker Order was the cause of her followers making use of the expression, "Christ made his second appearance in Ann Lee." Christ had appeared in thousands before our Mother lived, and also before the days of Jesus.

New truths have been revealed to the disciples of Mother Ann, from time to time, ever since the Shaker Order has been established. Our brother, Paul Tyner, is right in this. Fast upon the downfall of the generative life has come the enlightenment.

Creeds have fallen before the Star of Revelation. The Trinity is dethroned. God is our Heavenly Father and Mother. The atonement by the death of Jesus has passed away.

Baptism by water is supplanted by the baptism of fire and the Holy Spirit, the Christ. The spiritual fire is to consume the evils inherent in the human soul, the tares. "There is a fire in Zion, and a furnace in Jerusalem."

ELDRESS LIZZIE NOYES.

Sabbathday Lake, Maine.

"O brighter than the morning star
    Is the heart that is pure and free!
And the light that 's ever glowing there,
    The star of purity.
The sun shall wane, the stars go down,
    And reign of time be o'er,
But the living light in the heart that 's pure
    Shall shine forever more."

The Eucharist is understood to be received by living the pure life which Jesus lived—typified by the body and blood, which means the life.

Endless punishment is also routed, and an angry God is no more. But the sinner finds punishment enough. Each must atone for his own sins, by bringing them to the light and forsaking them forever. When reformation is complete, the punishment is removed.

Progression after death is also established—a travel of the soul from one degree of grace and glory to another for ever and ever. A soul can recede from God after death, yet the farther he gets away, the harder he will find it to return; but return he must sooner or later. Even the Parsees bring back their first old evil one, Ahriman and his rebellious host. After being purified by fire they all return and are forgiven.

In the Shaker Community woman has taken her place as an equal with man, by intellectual if not by physical strength. Where there is an Elder, there is also an Eldress; where there is a Deacon, there is a Deaconess, considered equal in their powers of government.

The Order is founded upon present revelation sustained by the inspired Word. God is as able and willing to reveal his will to man to-day as he was two thousand years ago. The Bible contains much that is inspired and much that is not, but God has placed his law in the hearts of his people.

A Shaker must live in the light, he must walk the

straight path of purity, and consecrate himself and all that he has to the upbuilding of the cause; should he depart from either of these principles he ceases to be a Shaker.

The arts and sciences, in a future day, will flourish under the patronage of those living the highest life, the Shaker life. Heretofore the work of drawing the lines between flesh and spirit has been so great that there has been no time to give to any other thought but that of watching all the avenues to keep out the evils that might enter and destroy the good that has been gained.

In the new heavens and new earth, all that is pure and elevating in art and the sciences will be understood and appreciated.

THY WILL BE DONE.

[From the *Manifesto*.]

Is there any reserve in this? And can "Thy kingdom come" unless the will of God is done? Are we able to take by violence and hold that heavenly kingdom, which we have so long been striving to obtain, and for which so many have fallen in the fearful struggle?

We believe that the Holy City, the New Jerusalem, hath come down from God, and we are privileged, spiritually, to walk its lovely streets. Here wrangling and confusion are very much out of place, and what would be our appearance in soiled and ragged garments? Our spiritual robes cannot be clean and white unless we live in purity in thought and deed.

We have been assured that there are angel bands who march through the heavens, and surround the throne of the Highest. How could these be held together unless there was perfect order, and each had his place assigned him and kept himself in it? Do they not cheerfully move in the spirit of "Thy will be done"? So we will cheerfully resign our spirits, and follow that "cloud by day and pillar of fire by night" which goes before the chosen people, as they travel away from the wilderness of sin. "The tabernacle of God is with man." Believing this, we find God in our union with his saints. Separate our spirits from them and we are lost, like wandering stars, in the regions of darkness.

"He that overcometh will I make a pillar in the temple of my God, and he shall go no more out; and I will write upon him a new name." This promise is for us if we are worthy; if not, others will take our places.

Our lives are required at our hands. Let us reserve nothing for self, but with full purpose of heart resolve to carry out, daily, a perfect consecration, and realize the hundred fold reward. "He that loseth his life for my sake shall find it," saith the Christ.

Mary Ella Douglass,

MARY ELLA DOUGLASS.

*Who left her companions at Sabbathday Lake for a more beautiful home
in the Spirit Land, February 9, 1893.*

"Sweet Summer Land, O Land of bright glory !
Thy beautiful fields are spread out before me ,
Thy verdant groves, and thy vineyards fair,
And my soul exclaims, ' How wonderful they are ! ' "

ANGELS OF THE NEW DISPENSATION.

[Read in our meeting for Soul Communion.]

Behold we come! Wafted upon the zephyrs from the Elysian fields we come unto you. Glory and brightness are in our wake, and the beautiful rivers of heavenly love are rolling onward, deluging the land from shore to shore.

Home of the favored and blest! Home of the pure and the true! We came unto you first; we came unto you in the early dawn, when the birds sang of this New Hope that is now being established by the scientific researches of the day.

Search your records, for laid away in your archives are thousands of messages, words of prophecy, of love, and of comfort, which we brought unto you before we went abroad to do our work with the nations of the earth. We will come unto you again. In God's good time we will come.

Hush! breathe not a thought of doubt while undergoing the throes of a mighty change. Not one jot nor one tittle of all that we have said unto you shall fail. Your banner shall be raised on high; higher than ever before shall be your standard, and your victory shall be acknowledged by the nations of the earth.

Children of the New Hope, look well to the path in which your feet are found to be walking, for on the plane of nature is the home of discord and strife. We can never walk with you there. But in the bower of purity and spiritual life you will find us. Here we will walk with you, and talk with you, and sing unto you the beautiful songs of the redeemed among men.

Listen and you shall hear our voices. Come near unto us and we will draw near unto you. We will feed you from our ambrosial stores, and clothe you in fine linen, clean and white. Come unto us all ye that labor and are heavy laden, and we will give you rest.

Amen and amen.

Lizzie and Hiram Bailey.

SOME OF OUR CHILDREN AND THEIR TEACHERS.

Samuel Kendrick.

LETTER TO THE EDITOR OF THE MANIFESTO.

November, 1889.

Elder Henry C. Blinn:—

You gave us from your diary in the November *Manifesto*, such a graphic account of your journey and visit to the Western Societies, that it almost seems that we went along with you on that delightful tour. You were very kind to write this up for us, and we thank you from our hearts.

The November *Manifesto* is very interesting to us. The music, "Beautiful Shore," awakens memories of loved ones who have gone on before, and are now enjoying the grandeur and beauty of that heavenly home; while our homes here are so vividly described that we cannot but feel how good it is to be joined to all that is lovely, pure, and true.

Now I must own that the lesson for the Bible class is what has drawn me out to write you this letter. It will be very interesting to read the answers to the questions, and I hope a goodly number of pupils will respond, and by so doing be a credit and honor to their kind teachers.

It seemed to me, good Elder Henry, while reading over these questions, that I would like to give you my ideas in regard to them, although they may greatly diverge from the opinions of others.

First answer: The two verses of Psalms, used as a prayer, that to me are the sweetest and strongest, are the tenth and the eleventh verses of the eighty-fourth Psalm: "For a day in Thy courts is better than a thousand," etc.

Second: Is there a more noble act of self-sacrifice recorded in the Old Testament than that made by Jephthah's daughter, when she yielded herself so willingly, that her father might keep the rash vow he had made unto the Lord?

Third: As the opinion of an individual, I would say that the grandest character in the Old Testament is the Prophet Daniel. The purity of his life was very nearly like that of Jesus. He lived the angel virgin life, approaching divinity. It seems that Joseph and Job were spotless characters, but they were upon the plane of nature.

Fourth: The Book of Daniel is to me the most interesting book of the Old Testament, notwithstanding Robert Elsmere tells us it is a fraud. In the last chapter is the sweetest prophecy of all: "Blessed is he that waiteth, and cometh to the thousand, three hundred and five, and thirty days." Has that time come? and is Daniel now standing in his lot, at the end of the days?

ELDER HENRY C. BLINN.

Bishop of the Societies in New Hampshire.

"Countless millions ages hence
Shall sing and speak the praise
Which fills the heart and moves the lips
Of saints in latter days."

Fifth: Matthew, eleventh chapter, commencing at the twenty-eighth verse: "Come unto me all ye that labor and are heavy laden, and I will give you rest," and so on, "and ye shall find rest unto your souls," with the conditions. What promise could be more comforting to the weary?

Sixth: Proverbs, thirteenth chapter, sixth and seventh verses, are very wise.

Seventh: The forty-fifth Psalm is most joyous, and very significant to the followers of Mother Ann Lee: "My heart is inditing a good matter," etc.

I must now come down from this height and write of home. In New Gloucester we have had an abundant crop of winter apples, very fair and free from defects. Many of these have been sold at a good price, but enough are stored with other fruits and vegetables for future use. Thus we are prepared to enter the cold season, happy in the anticipation of all temporal needs supplied, while the loving companionship of good Brothers and Sisters crowns the whole with joy unspeakable.

Home comforts are not the least of the many blessings bestowed upon us by our Heavenly Father and Mother.

TRIBUTE TO ELDER GILES B. AVERY.*

Brothers and Sisters in Christ:—

The great change which we all anticipate has come to our reverend Elder Giles. No more will he stand before us as of old, his countenance beaming with inspiration, hope and joy. But from those evergreen shores, by faith we still hear his voice and feel the same power from his overflowing spirit.

Long years ago, when very young, I remember hearing Elder Otis Sawyer say, "I have received a letter from an angel of the Lord."

"And who might that angel be?" was the question propounded.

He answered, "Giles B. Avery of Mount Lebanon, N. Y." That was before either of them took their later spiritual burdens.

By and by he stood before us as one of the leaders of our fair Zion, and the impression was strong: There

_____

*Of the Central Ministry, who passed away from earth December 27, 1890, at Watervliet, N. Y.

GILES B. AVERY.

" The Angel of the Lord."

I want to feel my spirit blest,
Find for my soul a home of rest,
And my union, pure and strong,
With the heavenly orders moving on.

G. B. A.

stands " the angel of the Lord." And so it has remained
up to this day.

> There is a land of pure delight,
>   It is not far away,
> And there, arrayed in garments white,
>   Our Elder walks to-day.
> He sends to us a blessing pure,
>   A message to abide,
> O Zion, thou wilt stand secure,
>   For God is on thy side.

LETTER TO COUNT LEO TOLSTOI.*

SABBATHDAY LAKE, MAINE, February, 1891.

Dear Friend and Brother :—

Here in America is a home prepared for those who desire to live pure lives, and the Christ spirit revealed through Ann Lee is the foundation thereof, and the spirits of the redeemed administer thereunto.

The indwellers of this home are now beholding a light on the distant horizon. It is the light from your stronghold, and it can never be quenched.

Your companion, in that she is sacrificing herself to sustain you in your convictions of right and in living them out, is largely endued with the spirit of Christ. We are thankful at every thought that you have such a help at your side, and also that your daughter Titiana is proving herself worthy of such a father.

In bringing to light the unfruitful works of darkness, you have gone to the depth of human depravity, as Ann Lee has done before you.

---

* This letter was suggested by reading the "Kreutzer Sonata," and was forwarded to Count Leo Tolstoi at Tula, Russia, by Brother Alonzo Holister of Mt. Lebanon, N. Y.

SISTERS OF THE COMMUNITY AT SABBATHDAY LAKE, MAINE.

"She stripped a carnal nature
        Of all its deep disguise,
And laid it plain and naked
        Before the sinner's eyes."

You have done the same, and the sinners of the nations are now in a squirming condition. The Word which went forth from Ann Lee one hundred years ago has now gone forth from you, and the trumpet gives no uncertain sound.

Ann Lee arose in the dawning of the morning and took upon herself the spirit of Christ, the same spirit that baptized the man Jesus. He was the first among many Brethren. She is the first among many Sisters. "And this is the name wherewith she shall be called, 'The Lord of our Righteousness.'"

The women of the nations are following in her wake, asserting themselves equal to their brothers, both in the sciences and governments. They will acknowledge her and confess her name when they find out the spirit that is leading them.

Jesus was administered to by the spirits of the just. He saw them. His disciples saw them. And you, dear friend, have a mighty host around you. They whisper to your spirit; you listen and write. They lay their hands of blessing upon you; you feel and receive.

God's people everywhere are sending you their love and encouragement.

Your sister is the cause of self-denial.

JESUS—BUDDHA—THE SERMON ON THE MOUNT.

[From the *Manifesto.*]

In *The Arena* for March, 1892, Charles Schroder asks the question, " Where do we find the Christian teachers of any sect, creed, or denomination, who dare to preach and live, or even accept this grand sermon in its entirety?" If he should visit the Shaker Communities, he would find a people who do accept the Sermon on the Mount as their guide, whose aim is to control their lives by its teachings in every respect. He would find in them some who are true followers of Jesus, The Christ, and who have in reality entered "The Path" and are walking the straight and narrow way.

During the six hundred years from Buddha to Jesus, spiritual light was increasing, and Friend Schroder is right in ranking the teachings of Buddha second to those of Jesus.

Both of these great teachers opened to the people a " Path, which the vulture's eye hath not seen. The lion's whelps have not trodden it, nor the fierce lion passed by it."

"Enter the path," said Buddha, to those who would become his followers (among them were some of his nearest relatives), when he returned from the wilderness, enlightened, illumined, and all animal passions subdued.

"Straight is the gate and narrow is the way which leadeth unto life, and few there be that find it," said Jesus.

In all the ages that are passed, how few there have been who have entered the straight and narrow way and turned neither to the right nor to the left, but kept onward and upward until they have reached the heights for which they started.

These, by the discipline brought to bear upon their daily lives, have found their spirits purified, all selfishness eradicated, and every evil passion subdued. That it can be done has been proved by loyal souls. If Friend Schroder will visit Mt. Lebanon, N. Y., East Canterbury, N. H., even our little home at Sabbathday Lake, Maine, or any of the Shaker Societies, he will find people who lift up their voices in denunciation of war, and all the evils of the day and also of the night.

It is not because their number is small that they are not heard. The multitude have blinded their own eyes and stopped their own ears. They will not see, they will not hear.

"THE SHAKERS AND THEIR HOMES."*

[From the *Manifesto*.]

SABBATHDAY LAKE, ME., February, 1893.

Brothers and Sisters of the Highest Life :—

From victory to victory in the path of purity you have walked from youthful days until the present time, and now as said the beloved apostle so can you say, "We know that we are of God, and the whole world lieth in wickedness."

Elder Giles B. Avery once said, "Zion is the working hands of God in the world." It then becomes the duty of believers to " sow light till the world is aglow." If we fail to do this, others may arise to take our birthright, and it is now evident that light is greatly needed to shine abroad over the earth.

Whenever we come in contact with those outside, we find that we are very imperfectly known unto them. The questions which meet us at every turn are like these : "What is your religious belief?" "What is the difference between you and the Quakers?" "Have you books that will inform us of your history and manner of life?"

---

*By Charles Edson Robinson.

OUR CHILDREN.

In answer to the last question, we tell them that we have books, large and small, and we have let them have a great many written by those of long spiritual travel and deep theological study and experience. Thousands will yet arise to call our good Father F. W. Evans blessed for the labors from his brain and pen, and also others who have toiled in the same field.

But "variety is the spice of life," and one outside of our homes has written an interesting series of articles, in a very friendly spirit, giving the history of the Order from its commencement; of the organization of the Societies, and the foundation principles by which they are governed; also biographical reminiscences, together with illustrations of nearly all our villages and some of our leading members. These articles have appeared during the last two years in the *Manufacturer and Builder*, a magazine published in New York City.

The work has been revised and very kindly given to us, with the use of the plates for the illustrations, by the writer of the series, our good friend, Charles Edson Robinson, who it seems has made the lives of God's people a study, and is himself not far from the kingdom.

At a sacrifice of time and labor the work is now being printed and put into book-form by Elder Henry C. Blinn, editor of the *Manifesto*. His reward is with him, to give unto the people according as their subscriptions to the books have been.

In our correspondence with the Brothers and Sisters

of the different Societies, in regard to the work, the kind
spirit in which we have been answered has filled our
hearts with thankfulness. We are particularly grateful
for the approval and help of the Elders of the North
Family, Mt. Lebanon. It is our hope and trust that in
the future new editions of and additions to this work
may be made, until "the knowledge of the Lord shall
cover the earth as the waters cover the sea." Even now
the tide of adversity is rolling back and prosperity's
waves are rolling in.

The Voice of the Spirit will be heard to the uttermost
parts of the earth.

> " For the angels are coming down from heaven,
>   To bless the people anew,
>   They are coming with rich and beautiful gifts
>   For every one of you."

ADDRESS TO THE SCHOOL AT SABBATHDAY LAKE.

I was made happy this afternoon by an invitation to visit your school. I find that it has been a very profitable term to you. The improvement that you have made is plainly to be seen. The teachers have done credit to themselves, and the pupils are a credit to their teachers.

All who have attended here this winter are not scholars, but all are pupils. Appearances show that the pupils have been trying very hard to become scholars.

Your school-days are slipping away, term after term.

In future years you will recall these days as the happiest period of your lives, and the very sight of an old book that you used in school will send a thrill of delight through your whole being.

As you advance in life, you will sense more and more the sacrifices that your teachers have made for you. Of these you can have but little idea now. I know the joys and the sorrows of a teacher's life. I know the hopes and the fears, and I know how the teacher enters into the little life of each child under her charge, and I know how it hurts her to take away your merits. But I hope

you have not lost your merits. I hope you are all entitled to prizes.

You are going out into the spring that will soon be
upon us. The mayflowers will bloom in the green pastures, the violets and buttercups will appear, and many
pleasures will be yours as you roam over the fields of
your beautiful home. While you are enjoying all this,
do not forget your school-lessons, but let them combine
to teach you to be good men and good women in all
your future years.

You have many friends who are watching you anx-
iously. You must not only be to them all that they
expect, but, if possible, you must be to them all that
they desire.

And now farewell for the present. I hope to meet
you here again in the lovely month of June. Then the
birds will be singing in a thousand tree-tops, and the
orchards and gardens will be blooming in beauty.

ATTENDING SHAKER MEETING, 1886.

INVOCATION.

"Will God dwell on the earth?"

Behold, the Heaven and the Heaven of Heavens can
not contain thee, how much less this house that has
been built unto thy name! Yet have thou respect unto
the prayers of thy people this day, that thine eyes may
be open towards this house in all coming time. For
thou hast said, "My name shall be there."

Our Heavenly Father and Mother, who sustained our
parents who have gone before, who opened a way for
them in the wilderness, and strengthened their hands to
build up this beautiful home for us to enjoy, grant that
this house that stands on the site of the one they reared
may be a continuation of the same, with an increase.

Hear thou the voice of prayer and praise which
ascends to thy throne this day, from thy consecrated
and devoted people.

Bless thou the spirits of the fathers and mothers who
have laid down their lives in this place.

And, O bless with a special blessing Elder Otis Sawyer, who went out from among us in the midst of his labors in the beauty and glory of heavenly light; whose spirit is now here, a watchful guardian, beaming with the brightness and joys of immortal youth.

And, O our Heavenly Father and Mother, grant that a double portion of thy blessing may rest upon our beloved leaders, the Ministry of the Bishopric in Maine. May the heavy burdens be lifted, and their spirits filled with joy unspeakable.

And all our loving Elders, hear thou from thy throne in the heavens, that the sunshine of thy love may abide with them forever.

Send thou a message of peace to the aged ones who meet here and renew the heart of each toiling brother and sister.

May this day long be remembered by every little child whose home is in the beautiful Zion of God in this place.

Amen and amen.

NEW YEAR'S GREETING.

[From the *Manifesto*.]

Brothers and Sisters of the Household of Faith:—

Our good Sister Ada S. Cummings, who writes our monthly notes for the *Manifesto*, has some trouble with her eyes and therefore must be careful for the present. As she cannot write until the time will be past for you to receive our New Year's greeting in the January number, I thought I would tell you that we at Sabbathday Lake wish you all a happy New Year.

It is a hazy Sabbath, not what we would call foggy, for the sun is shining almost through, and it makes us think that heaven is beyond only a little way. We attended our religious service and heaven appeared right in our midst, no haze to separate. Eldress Harriet Goodwin spoke beautifully to the youth and children, and said that she had noticed a marked improvement in their deportment, and this is what her loving motherly eye is quick to see. Their Elders and teachers spare no pains with them, and they show that they are giving good heed to the kind instruction which they receive from day to day.

This afternoon I visited Sister Ada and her company

of little girls. They were just arranging for a meeting of their own. I asked if I could be a spectator, and liberty was granted at once. They had leaders appointed from their own number, and the order was perfect. The gifts of the spirit were really made manifest.

Toward the close of the meeting I taught them the "Celestial March" and other religious exercises, which made the worship of our fathers and mothers so beautiful; and that caused me to think of the pure and holy lives which our fathers and mothers lived. O how white and clean are the spiritual robes of the children of the resurrection!

These are Sabbathday notes and temporal matters are left out. So in the commencement of the New Year we will seek the spiritual first, then the temporal blessings will be added.

ELDRESS HARRIET GOODWIN.

Of the Maine Ministry.

Round my heart I feel entwining tendrils of the sweetest love,
Bearing me from things terrestrial to the brighter spheres above.

H. G.

WINTER.

[From the *Manifesto*.]

" 'T is done ! Dread Winter spreads his latest glooms,
And reigns tremendous o'er the conquered year."

What is that to us? We but slightly feel its effects, hived together as we are in our pleasant dwellings, enjoying the hoarded increase of our broad fields, our gardens, orchards and vineyards. We saw the spring, summer and autumn pass away, while joys and sorrows alternately filled our cup. We mingled our tears when affliction's wave rolled over, and exulted together in the blissful hour.

Pleasant memories arise of much that we have enjoyed in the year that has passed, particularly, those seasons when our brothers and sisters visited us from other Societies of Believers. You came to see us from your beautiful homes, and with you came a blessing that passeth not away with the onward flow of time.

We remember when we united in songs of praise in the sanctuary, and the word went forth for judgment and mercy to all who would listen, from far and near. We remember pleasant walks over this consecrated domain,

7

and rides over the hills and dales of the neighboring towns. Those days are passed, but the joy remaineth.

A good aged father, Albert Battles, from the Society of Enfield, Conn., visited us in the beautiful month of June, and in a social meeting sang of his great love to Mother Ann Lee, who held aloft the standard of purity, and revealed principles which are now widely accepted. We were awakened to a realizing sense of the vastness of her mission, overthrowing creeds, and establishing theories which cannot be shaken by the increase of light in the world, nor the forward march of science.

> " O my mother, my blessed mother,
>   Her name to me is dear;
> I 'll praise her name, I 'll spread her fame,
>   And kings and priests shall hear.
> There 's many thousands praised her name,
>   And shall be many more;
> Yea, millions, millions, tens of millions
>   Shall her name adore."

Father James Whittaker, when a young man in England, saw a vision of the Order that was yet to be established in America, and it was like unto a beautiful tree— every leaf thereof shone with the brightness of the sun. Those leaves are gems of priceless worth, held in place by the branches, receiving nourishment from the root, drawing life from the atmosphere around, the rain, the dew and the sunshine of the heavens. Those leaves are my brothers and sisters inhabiting the Zion of God, clothed with the love and growing in the likeness of our Heavenly Parents.

In worship, I have seen them pass and re-pass each other like the angels, singing :—

> " 'T is the kind words, 't is the sweet words,
> That cheer the down-hearted,
> That lift up the spirit
> From doubt and despair.
> O then I will speak them
> Unto you, my brother !
> I 'll breathe forth a blessing
> To you, my dear sister."

VISIT TO THE SOCIETY AT ALFRED.

[From the *Manifesto*.]

SABBATHDAY LAKE, ME., November, 1896.

Beloved Elder Henry :—

I write to tell you of my visit to Alfred in the days of the Indian summer, from the twenty-fourth to the thirty-first of October.

By the Portland and Rochester train we were brought directly overland, in plain sight of the village, around the east side of the beautiful Massabesic Lake, to Alfred Corner, two miles from our destination. Here we were met by Brother Frank Libby and Eldresses Harriet Goodwin and Eliza R. Smith, with a carriage to take us home.

It was a lovely ride along the lakeside, the autumnal foliage decking the forests as far as the eye could see, amid slight zephyrs, the thought of which was just sufficient to fan away all earthly cares. In the society of those we love, how quickly time passes! We soon arrive at the office. Here we find Sister Lucinda Taylor waiting to receive us, and by her kindness and that of those with her all our needs are anticipated and ministered unto.

And now a thought of the sudden change—a week to

ELDER HENRY G. GREEN.

Alfred, York County, Maine.

" There is a kingdom forever increasing
    Where robes of redemption are worn,
Where the sun of righteousness beaming
    Createth an eternal morn.
I am winning that kingdom so holy,
    I am weaving those garments so fair,
Enshrouding my soul in bright glory,
    As the cross through life's burdens I bear."

rest from the cares and burdens incident to home life, that, during the past season, from the rush of business, was almost overpowering. Instead of caring for others, all are striving to care for you.

Upon the Sabbath we met for divine service. Prominent in the assembly were our venerable Elders, Joshua Bussell and Hiram Tarbox, in spirit firm as the hills, bearing the same testimony that we have often heard from them in the days that are past, both here and in our home at Sabbathday Lake. Beloved and consecrated ones, your spiritual children will reap in joy what you have sown in tears.

I cannot tell you of all the joys of those days, for space will not permit, but I will speak of the willow trees that I went to see one afternoon. They grew by the side of the old road over which Father James Whittaker came when he visited Alfred in the year 1785. He, and the Elders with him, stuck the withes that they had driven their horses with into the ground. They took root and grew to be these great trees, nearly three feet in diameter. The one that Father James set has fallen, and from the side of the trunk three or four large willows are growing. These will be succeeded by others. The root will not die out and, as the willow trees grow on and on, the seeds of eternal truth which Father James planted in this place will also grow. Those principles will never die. These were my thoughts as I stood upon the log of the fallen willow on that lovely afternoon.

In the cemetery we saw the names of the fathers and mothers who gave themselves, with all they had, to found this home for those who would follow in their footsteps, and live the high and pure life required of the sons and daughters of God. The final consecration was made when the Society was organized in the year 1793. Here they spent the remainder of their lives, living together as brothers and sisters, sharing equally in every temporal blessing. I noticed the names John Barnes, Elisha Pote, Rebecca Hodgdon, and many others. Names to be remembered in all coming time by those who tread the straight and narrow way which they marked out. Their lives were not in vain. "The stone that smote the image became a great mountain and filled the whole earth."

I returned to my home at Sabbathday Lake on Saturday, the thirty-first. Elder Henry G. Green, of the Alfred Society, came also, and we had the blessing of his presence over the Sabbath, and several days following. The young receive encouragement, and the weak in faith are strengthened by his steadfast spirit.

As I have in mind at this time, the home at Alfred, "Beautiful for situation," and also the home at Sabbathday Lake, I exclaim with the prophet, "How goodly are thy tents, O Jacob, and thy tabernacles, O Israel! As the valleys are they spread forth, as gardens by the river's side, as the trees of lign-aloes which the Lord hath planted, and as cedar trees beside the waters."

"CEDARS OF LEBANON."

Members of the Community at Mount Lebanon, Columbia County, N. Y.   Elder Evans in the Center.

TO THE CEDARS OF LEBANON.

"The Lord is in his holy temple; let all the earth keep silence before him."

"His foundation is in the holy mountains."

Therefore "my heart is inditing a good matter." It is of the "Mount Lebanon Cedar Boughs," a book the literature of which is of the highest type, gems of poetic genius, written by the Queen's Daughters, whose clothing is of wrought gold. By them it is dedicated not only to the household of faith, but to all yearning souls in the wide, wide world.

They are boughs from the Cedars of Lebanon. The trees are still there, waving in grandeur and beauty. They are poems sent forth to enlighten and educate, and to make manifest the intellectual power that has been attained in the spiritual communistic life. Under no other condition can a door be open for such a pure and refined education as that acquired in the home that has peen prepared, whose foundation is in the holy mountain.

Here in this favored retreat minds have been disciplined until sordid desires have been subdued, selfishness destroyed, and the animal nature overcome. From this altitude they look upon the children of men, ever ready to lend a helping hand to draw them up to higher and purer lives. It is to this cause they give their strength from day to day, and as they give, they renew their strength from the overflowing fountain of God's love. They walk and do not faint, they run and do not weary.

Here also is found that mine of intellectual wealth from which these Cedar Boughs have emanated. We read one poem; it is beautiful, and we want to call your attention to it. We read another; it is equally good, and so on, from the beginning to the end of the book.

The Mother in the Deity is here made manifest. The Mother Spirit in the New Creation here stands in her place. The virgins that follow her are brought unto the King in raiment of needlework; with gladness and rejoicing they come, for grace is poured into their lips. They ride prosperously, because of truth and meekness and righteousness.

Thus the Cedars of Lebanon wave in majesty, distilling dew and sending forth "boughs" for the healing of the nations.

The Daughters of Zion have arisen to thresh and to beat in pieces many peoples, and they will " consecrate their gain unto the Lord, and their substance unto the Lord of the whole earth."

Amen, so let it be.

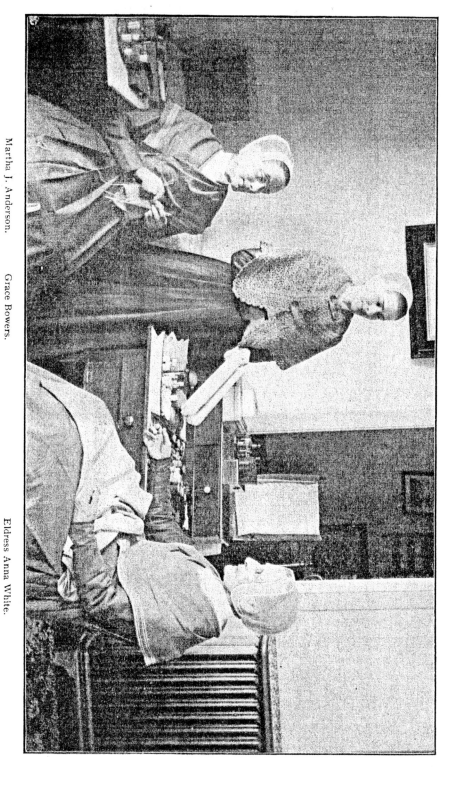

Martha J. Anderson.   Grace Bowers.   Eldress Anna White.

"THE QUEEN'S DAUGHTERS IN RAIMENT OF NEEDLEWORK."

Mount Lebanon, Columbia County, N. Y.

DEDICATION AT POLAND SPRINGS OF THE MAINE STATE BUILDING.*

ALSO THE CELEBRATION OF THE CENTENNIAL OF THE RICKER FAMILY AS HOTEL PROPRIETORS IN THE TOWN OF POLAND, ME., JULY 1st, 1895.

The day was seemingly made for the occasion. It was a beautiful day when the great men of the State of Maine met upon her loveliest spot of ground.

The Shakers had been kindly invited by the proprietors to be present, and be assured we availed ourselves of the privilege.

A number of our people went early and had front seats. Our carriage came a little later and stopped in the road opposite. We were near enough to hear distinctly all that was said, and see the speakers upon the platform.

We heard the governor of the State, Honorable Henry B. Cleaves, deliver an able address. The next speaker was a Judge Advocate-General of Massachusetts.

---

* Removed from the World's Columbian Exposition Grounds at Chicago, Ill., and re-erected in the grove near the Poland Spring House by Hiram Ricker & Sons.

Senator Eugene Hale was then introduced. I would like to tell you all that he said, but can only give you a small portion. He apostrophized the building, and said to it, "My young friend, if you are wise and sensible stay right where you are and thank the Lord that you are out of Chicago. You ought to feel like a man who has just emerged from an election riot in the lower streets of New York City, and has launched himself into the placidity of a Shaker meeting here in the State of Maine. You ought to be glad that you are rid of noise, and temptation, and anarchists, my young friend, and that you have come down here where Nature sits at her best, and broods lovingly over such a scene as human eyes have rarely witnessed."

He then spoke of what the Rickers had done here in the past and in the present. He said: "They do everything in a delightful way—do it handsomely, do it well. They are great benefactors. Talk about the discovery of America in 1492, I am inclined to think that Hiram Ricker, who discovered this spring, was a greater benefactor than Christopher Columbus. The man who is able to give us a good digestion, sleep all night, and that perpetual serenity which the old English essayists talk about, does more good than the man who discovers a country."

Senator Hale said much more, equally interesting and true, when Senator William P. Frye took the stand. He kept the people laughing, and the applause was so great that we could hardly hear what he said; but we know the mothers and sisters of the Ricker family were brought in for their share of the honors of building up this beautiful place. God bless him for this! And he spoke of another mother, whose home was in sight upon another hill like unto this, who reared up so many of the great men of the nation, namely, the Washburns. Thus he held the people entranced throughout the length of his speech.

The next speaker was Hon. Nelson Dingley, Jr. We listened spellbound to his glowing words, but his discourse was altogether too short, for it was but a few minutes before the chairman introduced Hon. Charles A. Boutelle, of Bangor, Maine, Member of Congress.

In the course of his speech he, in a vein of mirthfulness, mentioned Massachusetts as once being a part of Maine. He said: "We are proud of Massachusetts. We are glad of what she has achieved with the assistance which we have given her from time to time. We are glad that we have furnished her her best Governors, such as Andrew and Long. We are proud that we have given her her merchant princes," etc. His words sent a thrill of delight through the audience, especially those who were natives of Maine. We were glad to be reminded of how much the dear old State of Maine had to be proud of in her daughter, Massachusetts.

The last speaker was Gen. A. P. Martin, of Boston. He kept up the interest by a fine flow of oratory. His native place was about three miles distant, in New Gloucester. He loved these hills and dales, over which he roamed in the days of his boyhood. He quoted poetry, and his themes were grand and beautiful.

The dinner hour had now arrived, and all were called to a sumptuous repast, such as only can be found at the Poland Spring Hotel, given freely by the proprietors to the hundreds of people who were upon the ground that lovely day.

Thus passed one of the most pleasant seasons in our existence. Not only was the dedication of the Maine building a complete success, but the centennial of the Ricker family as hotel proprietors in Poland was made prominent by each of the speakers.

A little over one hundred years ago, Eliphaz Ring, the Shaker, owned this hill with the broad fields and wood-lands bordering on the lakes. He owned the spring, and drank its healing waters without a thought. Little did he imagine what the future would develop. But it was not for him nor his posterity. He heard and obeyed the call to a higher life, when the Shakers held meetings in these homes, commencing in November 1783. He occupied his home here with his family until the time of the organization of the Shaker Society at Alfred, Maine, in 1793. Our Society at Sabbathday Lake was organized under the same leadership, the 19th of April, 1794, as was stated in a former chapter.

Jabez Ricker, ancestor of these proprietors, owned one

MAINE STATE BUILDING.
In the grove near the Poland Spring House, South Poland, Maine.

of the farms where the Society at Alfred is located. He owned the mill privilege. By an act of kindness to the Shakers, he consented to exchange farms with Eliphaz Ring, and moved his family to this hill and here opened a hotel one hundred years ago. By this bargain the Shakers in Alfred came into possession of their valuable mill-privilege, and some of their richest lands between the beautiful lakes, Massabesic and Bunganut.

Eliphaz Ring moved his family to Alfred about this time, and they were among the leading members of the Shaker Society while they lived. I think that none of them turned back to the old way.

Ruth, a daughter of Eliphaz, had married Thomas Cushman of Buckfield, Maine. They became Shakers, and went to Alfred with the Ring family. They had two sons. One of them chose the Shaker life, and became a highly-respected member and Elder in the Alfred Society. The other son remained outside, and is the ancestor of some of the nicest people in Auburn, Maine.

Thomas Cushman was the financial leader of the Alfred Society a number of years. He afterwards became Bishop of the three Societies in Maine. He was loved by all the people, but they had to part with him. He died in the year 1816, being only fifty-seven years of age. His successor was Elisha Pote, of whom mention has been made in this book.

The Society at Gorham, Maine, moved to the southern Rang Hill, one mile from Poland Springs, in 1819. In

1887 it was merged into the Society at Sabbathday Lake.

Thus we see that God's ways, though to us inscrutable at the time, have in these cases finally brought good to all concerned.

THE SHAKER SETTLEMENTS OF CANTERBURY AND ENFIELD, N. H.

[From the *Manifesto.*]

It was a lovely morning—October 22d, 1897—when Elders William Dumont and Henry Green, Eldress Elizabeth Haskell and the writer started from Alfred, Maine, for a visit to the Societies of Believers in New Hampshire. Through a clear, crisp atmosphere the smoking engine hurried us along over hill and through dale, by pleasant woodlands and cultivated farms to Alton Bay. Then for a number of miles along the shores of Lake Winnipiseogee, through whose clear, placid waters could be plainly seen the white, pebbly bottom of the lake. One view of Mt. Washington, far to the north-west, and we are off to Laconia, at which station we are made glad by meeting two brethren from Canterbury, Elders Benjamin Smith and Arthur Bruce, with carriages to take us to their pleasant village, twelve miles distant. We arrive as the shades of evening are falling, and are welcomed to one of our most beautiful homes by our own Brothers and Sisters. All things needed for our comfort are amply provided by their love and care. The

days of our visit come and go, all pleasant days, bringing pleasures and surprises manifold.

In the office of the *Manifesto*, our beloved Elder,
Henry C. Blinn explains to us the machinery by which
our thoughts are stamped upon paper, and the little
pamphlets are made which carry our ideas to the Societies of Believers and to the outside world; all done under his watchful guidance. He then took us to his
museum, where are carefully stored many relics of old,
so interesting to us in these latter days. We saw the
skeleton in the closet, reminding us that we are "fear-
fully and wonderfully made," and while these earthly
forms are moldering in the dust, the spirit, which is the
reality, is marching on in the beautiful life beyond.

We are visiting with those we long have loved, and
are surrounded by scenes which call to mind historical
events of the old times. Not the least of these is the
building in which the Sacred Roll was printed in the
year 1843. Before us we seem to see Philemon Stewart
in all the glory of his great inspiration. Of our company, only one can remember those days.

The evenings are delightfully enjoyed. One evening
we listened to the quartet, to the piano and organ, the
next to the orchestra; but the evening in which the pilgrims marched to the Holy City was the entertainment
which took the palm. We saw the beautiful city with its
battlements and towers. We saw the shining ones passing out and in, guiding the pilgrims along their weary

DAVID PARKER.

Formerly Trustee, East Canterbury, N. H.

" Not all a dream, a passing dream,
    Is Life's unfoldment here ;
Earth's brightest glories are but gleams
    From out the inner sphere.
What hopes and longings fill the heart,
    And lift the mind on high—
They tell that the immortal part
    Can never, never die."

way. We saw Doubt and Scorn and all the powers of evil vanquished. Then the door was opened to receive them, amid the rejoicing of the angels.

Under the loving control of Eldress Dorothy A. Durgin these entertainments are perfected and carried out. The magnetism of her spirit smooths down the roughness, always strengthening the weak and drawing out the good. It is the divine Mother Spirit in her, personified.

> " Beauty reigns all around thy borders,
>   Where her lovely feet have trod ;
>   Peace and order, love and union,
>   In the power and gift of God."

As time passes on the Sabbath comes. This day is marred by no cloud. It is a perfect day. At the appointed hour the sanctuary is opened, not only for the Believers, but also for those friends who choose to attend. The singing is in perfect harmony, and most beautiful and inspiring.

In this service we had the privilege of listening to a discourse from Brother T. A. Dwyer, late from the outside churches, and now established in the New Jerusalem which hath come down from God out of heaven. The Word is held forth in perfect language, and as the testimony of true Shakerism falls from his lips, we cannot wonder that the two thousand who listened to his pleading tones in the Universalist church in Laconia, turned to their homes in tears of joy and new resolves for the

s

future. Thus will the old heavens and earth pass away and all things become new. This day came to a close like the others, and it will never be forgotten.

In the course of the coming week, Elder Henry C. Blinn and Eldress Emeline Hart conducted us to their home in Enfield. Eldress Joanna Kaime met us at the door, and her kind welcome gave us the assurance that we were not among strangers, but with our near and dear relations. Great kindness is shown to us in this home, where Elder Abraham Perkins spent so many years of his devoted life, the home of his heart's deep love.

We remained nearly a week in this beautiful place. Visited the North Family, which was the home of Elder John Lyon, that great expounder, who kept the sieve full and kept it shaking. Would that he were here now, to continue the work until the deserted villages were filled with the "Elect," "sought out and chosen."

The scenery here is magnificent. The brethren of our company went to a lake far up the mountain, on the west, fifteen hundred feet above the level of the village, from which the Society is always sure of an abundant supply of water. It seems to be in the crater of an old volcano, and there is no danger that it will ever break away and damage property.

Elder William Wilson very kindly took us around Mascoma Lake, east of the village, pointed out the spot where the first Shaker meeting was held in New Hamp-

LUCY ANN SHEPARD.

Trustee, East Canterbury, N. H.

" As the dew of the morning, or as bright rivers roll,
So freely God's blessings flow into my soul.
I walk in his presence as one greatly blest,
On whose soul the love of his work is impressed "

shire, where the home of James Jewett, the first convert, was situated, and where John Cotton received faith, he being the first one to bring the gospel testimony, after the order of our Church, into the State of Maine. That meeting was held the 8th of September, 1782.

We stopped a day over our time that we might meet Eldress Rosetta Cummings and Sister Caroline Whitcher, and three young Sisters who were absent from home. We enjoyed a lovely visit with them in the afternoon. In the evening we had our farewell visit with the Ministry and Elders, only for the present, however; many meetings are to be in the future.

The next day we were taken to the station by Brother George Baxter, and, saying farewell to him until our next meeting, we retraced our way to Canterbury. When we arrived in Concord the rain was falling in gentle showers. Elder Henry Green left us at this point for Boston, homeward bound. We were expecting Sister Lucy Ann Shepard and a company of Sisters from Canterbury, who were on their way to Boston. We enjoyed an hour's visit with these loved ones, and then went on to Canterbury with the young brethren, leaving the sisters to take the train. When we drove up to the office, many anxious ones were there to meet us; although the rain was pouring, the quartet was out, singing of the "patter, patter of the rain."

One day more in lovely Canterbury, which is to be well improved. We are granted another short visit with our dearly loved Sister Asenath Stickney, who is suffering from injuries received from a severe fall; also an additional visit with Sister Harriet Hastings, whom we have all known to love. Then we enjoy a delightful season with Elder Abraham Perkins, and tell him of our visit to his home in Enfield. He bears up remarkably under his ninety years.

By the kindness of our Canterbury friends, Sister Edna E. Fitts is to accompany us to our home at Sabbathday Lake, stay with us during the winter and teach music. The last morning arrived, and with Sister Edna we were taken to the station in Laconia. Here we part with Elder Benjamin and Elder Arthur, who have been so kind to us, and are on our way home. We stop at Alfred over night, and go on to Sabbathday Lake the next day. All is well. We again take up the thread of life in the old accustomed way. Our music teacher arranges her classes and commences her labor of love. Music is in the atmosphere and a song of rejoicing in our souls,—a song that can only be learned by the hundred forty and four thousand. The half has not been told.

THE DAY OF JUDGMENT.

THE light, at first a glimmer
   Along the eastern way,
Is beaming forth in splendor
   The dawning of the day.
White mists, like billowy mountains,
   From water-courses rise,
And sparkling with the sunbeams,
   Blend with ethereal skies.

Throughout the gloom and darkness
   We kept the vestal light,
And heard the voice from Seir,
   "Watchman, what of the night?"
"Behold the morning cometh,
   The Mighty One is here."
Was sounded from the watch-tower,
   "The Judgment Day is near."

O not as ye expected
   Does Gabriel's trumpet sound!
The still, small voice, in whispers,
   Is heard by all around.
O not as ye expected
   Does Christ through heaven ride!
The Living God is in you,
   You can not turn aside.

And not as ye expected
   Will Christ atone for you;
The light which now ariseth
   Will search you through and through.
Upon the vestal altars
   The holocaust is slain,
And fires thereon are burning
   The pride of man to stain.

And not as ye expected
   Will all the dead arise;
The dead in sin are hastening
   To make the sacrifice.
The bruised reed is strengthened,
   The sick and lame are healed
And to the feast invited,—
   The Book is now unsealed.

Come ye unto the banquet,
   The door no man can close,
And war has been proclaimed
   Against inherent foes.
With Michael's mighty army
   Defy the man of sin.
O not as ye expected
   The Judgment Days rolls in!

THE STORY OF GRANVILLE MERRILL, WHICH IS AN ACCOUNT OF ONE OF THE MIRACLES OF THE AGE.

Granville Merrill was a man of God.

He became a member of the Shaker Society at the age of twenty-nine years.

Nathan Merrill, who was the first person that embraced Shakerism in New Gloucester, Maine, was his great-grandfather. That was in November, 1783. He was a brick mason, and went to Alfred to help the people there build chimneys. It happened to be at the time that the Shaker ministers arrived with John Cotton from Enfield, N. H.

Many of the Alfred and Gorham people became Shakers. Prominent among them was Elisha Pote. His father's home was here in New Gloucester, also his brother Samuel's. Their two farms are included in this property.

Nathan Merrill, with Elisha Pote, who afterwards became the Presiding Elder of the Societies in Maine, and some others came here and held meetings—Elisha did the preaching.

Nathan Merrill was the first to accept the faith. Then his family and many others became Shakers. This has all been recorded and need not be repeated here.

In one of the first years Nathan's son Amos and one of the Shaker sisters, Mary Twombly, fell away and were married. They were the parents of Hiram Merrill, the father of Granville.

There was more or less Shaker faith in all those who turned away, and their descendants inherited in a measure the same spirit.

Granville's grandmother, who was Mary Twombly, when she was quite aged, came here to see the aged sisters, who were the companions of her girlhood days. They wept together. She said, "I wish you had not allowed me to go, I wish you had tied me in the old wash-house garret." The sisters said, "You did not feel in that way then."

Granville Merrill was born January 22d, 1839, in New Gloucester, Maine, about two miles south of Shaker village.

The neighborhood was in a low state morally. He was taught to smoke tobacco when only three years of age. Men would come to his father's house to spend social evenings and almost always had their liquor. Granville's father had him carry round the glasses and treat the company, and gave him a little for himself, which, he said, would slip down easily. Of course there was more or less drunkenness, with its attendant evils.

ELDER JOSEPH HOLDEN.

Of the Central Ministry, Mount Lebanon, N. Y.

United in bonds of one sweet communion,
Worldliness bears no charm for souls,
Riches will perish with all earthly treasures,
While spiritual life will always remain.

J. H.

In this atmosphere Granville lived and moved and had his being until he arrived at manhood.

When about nineteen years of age he was hired by the Shakers. Worked for them nearly ten years before he thought of being a Shaker. He had a pleasant disposition, was honest and a faithful workman. Towards the last of that time he was married, and had a child who was not born until after he became a Shaker.

When he was about twenty-eight years of age, he was what is called converted, in a revival meeting that was held near his home, and became a praying Christian.

When asked which denomination he intended to join, he said he did not know. He would read the New Testament and see what Jesus said, and join the church that came the nearest to the teachings of Jesus.

So he read, and the more he read the clearer he saw that the Shakers were living the life laid down in the New Testament. Now came the struggle. Whenever he prayed, the promise he had made would rise up before him. Then he would stop praying and suffer from a condemned conscience.

He went on in this way several weeks, until he could bear it no longer. He knew it was the call of God to him to sacrifice all worldly pleasures and enter the straight and narrow way and become one of the sons of God.

Now when his mind was made up he testified his faith both publicly and privately, and commenced to use the simple " yea " and " nay " of believers.

It was a fearful trial to his wife. He made every effort to bring her over to his way of thinking. In this he failed and she became the foe of his household. He gave her his earnings, which amply supplied all she needed for herself and the child. They owned a little place free and clear, which now she enjoyed by herself while he took up his abode with the brethren.

After a while she sued for a divorce, alleging that her husband had joined the Shakers. The divorce was granted, for which Granville paid the costs. He also gave her the place and one hundred dollars in money.

He now considered himself free and gave all his interests to the people of his choice, and became fully consecrated to the Cause of Believers.

He never saw his little boy after this. The child soon went to live with his grandparents on the mother's side. She went away and in due course of time was married again. Her maiden name was Anna Partridge.

Thus our brother bade adieu to his wife and child and all worldly relations. His testimonies were crisp and pointed. On one occasion he said these words:

"I have entered the straight and narrow way and will turn neither to the right nor to the left. By the help of God every evil shall go under my feet."

He made his first confession in the presence of Alonzo Gilman, who was at that time the novitiate Elder. As Granville's home was in the lower village, he was one mile away from where Elder Alonzo was stationed at Poland Hill. .

One day he went up to do this momentous work. Elder Alonzo happened at that time to be very busily engaged in hand labor, and could not attend to him. The burden did not fall from his shoulders at the foot of the cross, like that of Bunyan's Pilgrim. He had to take it back home and wait for another opportunity. He went up the next day and again found Elder Alonzo too busy to give him his attention. So he brought the burden back. In two or three days he went up the third time and found Elder Alonzo prepared, and the burden fell from his shoulders. He had carried it up that steep hill to the foot of the cross three times, but the releasement was to him a sure reward.

It was only temporal labor that hindered Alonzo from attending to that most sacred duty. That was not right. The spiritual should always come first. But the trial did not hurt Granville.

From this day his walk was straight and every indulgence cut off. As required of all believers, he put his hands to work and gave his heart to God.

It was a shock to his constitution to leave off tobacco, which he had always used, but by a strong will power he accomplished the feat, and never indulged in that vile weed from the day he started in the self-denying way until he closed this life.

Up at four o'clock in the morning to his work at the

mill or wherever it might be. Breakfast with the brethren at six and right back to his work, no lingering in the waiting-room. To dinner in the same way. No nooning. Ready for the meeting in the evening, always in possession of a spirit determined for the right and the right alone. Pleasant and cheerful through all that might arise to cloud the day. Ready and willing to go here and there when desired to make repairs, wherever they were needed. Thus he was always found to be the same kind brother.

He began missionary work soon after he came in. There was a young man living in the family of our next neighbor. His name was William Dumont, nineteen years of age. Though of a lively disposition, he was of a thoughtful turn of mind. Our aged Elder Joseph Brackett said one day, "William Dumont would make a good Shaker, and I will get him if I can." Granville made answer: "I have thought the same thing and will do all I can to help draw him out from the sea." He then began with prayers and spiritual labors whenever an opportunity presented itself. He was very persistent, and the work soon began to have an effect.

After a while our young brother acknowledged hearing the call to a higher life. Then the struggle commenced, for he had been promised a vessel and was to be the captain. He had many misgivings and finally came to the conclusion that he could live the higher life outside and not bind himself to this community.

WILLIAM DUMONT.

Sabbathday Lake, Maine.

" The pearl of true worth, the gift of salvation
Is free for all who the price will pay,
A fullness of spiritual beauty and glory,
O'ershadows the pilgrim's upward way."

When Granville found where he stood he gave him a searching look and said, "They that are not for us are against us, and they that gather not with us scatter abroad."

Thus our young brother found every weapon taken from his hands, and made up his mind to a full consecration.   In this he has remained faithful to this day, and is now the leading elder of the Societies in Maine, our Elder William Dumont.

Granville was always doing good works, and works that followed him.   He was a first-class mechanic.   Made with his own hands a large clock and hung it at the top of one of the buildings.   To-day, it can be heard striking nearly two miles away, and is doing the full duty for which it was designed.   Granville manufactured the machinery.   All that had to be bought in its make-up did not come to five dollars.   He also manufactured a small steam engine, which has been in use every year since for many things, mostly to prepare the poplar wood shavings for weaving the sisters' basket-work.

Thus a few years passed when it was noticed that his health was failing.   This brought anxiety and sorrow on all his loving brethren and sisters.

Knowing he must have a change of employment, they had him take the sisters' fancy work to the hotels at Bar Harbor, Orchard Beach and other places, and make sales.   In this he was very successful, and seemed to gain in health.   But the gain was of short duration.

With breaking hearts we saw that he was slowly and surely passing away from earth.

Thinking it might be that the sudden change from tobacco and other things that he was accustomed to had been too much of a shock to his constitution, it was proposed to him to use a little tobacco. "Nay," said he, "I will never put another piece of tobacco into my mouth." "Not if you knew it would save your life?" said Eldress Hester Ann Adams. "Not if I knew it would save my life," was his answer. "I will keep the promise I have made to God."

In the spring of 1878 he was obliged to take his room, being finally brought down by an abscess on his back, which made sure work taking his life away.

The same spirit of purity and brotherly love continued to the last. He had a thought for his little boy, who was cared for by outside relatives. But the child was taken sick and died the February before. Granville had proposed to take him under his own care when he arrived at the age of ten years. But the death of the child and his own sickness intervened. And the little spirit was ready for his father's kind care in the beautiful life beyond, which we fully believe he received.

On his bed of suffering our beloved brother was surrounded by loving friends. He saw their sorrow and their tears. "Grieve not for me," he said, "I will not leave you. I will be with you in spirit. Your interest will ever be mine, I will see that you have some one else to take my place." We well know that he has fulfilled this promise.

On the morning of the fourth of July, 1878, came the silence. We had to realize all we had expected. It was a beautiful morning when, in the midst of the nation's rejoicing, he, who had ruled his own spirit, arose in majesty, conqueror of the world and of death.

We had a beautiful meeting, called by some "a funeral," on the afternoon of the fifth of July. Then the outward form of our brother was laid away in our little cemetery. He is not there.

He passed from our sight at the age of thirty-nine years, five months and thirteen days.

The following elegy was read for him in our meeting:

TO OUR ARISEN BROTHER, GRANVILLE MERRILL.

> Come, a voice is calling loudly,
>   Come away, thy work is done.
> Come, thy cares and toils are ended,
>   And thy earthly race is run.
> Brother, thou hast borne with pleasure
>   All that was allotted thee ;
> Thou hast won a heavenly treasure
>   In the land of purity.
>
> Beauty blooms all round the mansion
>   Which is thine forever more,
> And the mountains rise in grandeur.
>   On that bright, eternal shore,
> Trees of life are growing upward,
>   Beams of glory rolling down,
> And the angel harps attuneth
>   In sweet praise of thy renown.

When, midst youthful strength and vigor
     Worldly pleasures promised thee,
Thou didst hear the Saviour calling:
     " Leave thou all and follow me,"
Didst thou turn aside with sorrow?
     Didst thou close thine eyes and ears?
Leave the bitter cup untasted?
     Yield to stoic doubts and fears?

Nay, thy life was freely given,
     All thou hadst without reserve,
Every tie of nature riven,
     God to worship and to serve.
Wife and child, upon the altar
     Spared thou not nor worldly kin,
Thou didst turn away from Sodom,
     Turn away from every sin.

Thou hast trod the road of straightness
     Followed Christ along the way,
Till this path has led thee upward
     To a bright unclouded day,
Now, new scenes are ope before thee
     And thy angel guides are near,
Mighty hosts of God's redeemed,
     Lo, we feel their presence here.

Soothing all our bitter sorrow,
     Giving peace, no tongue can tell,
Teaching us that God is holy
     And He doeth all things well;
Teaching us to bow in spirit,
     To be reconciled in truth,
That we may the prize inherit,
     Each, the aged and the youth.

Now, we hear, in gentle whispers,
     Voices which to us are dear,—
Voices, which are saying sweetly,
     Know, thy brother standeth near;

ELDER JOSEPH BRACKETT.

Our aged Father, who entered the land of rest July, 1882, being 85 years of age.

"Oh the beauty of that land!
How divine and glorious,
Where the saints in triumph stand
Singing songs victorious,
There through vernal bowers of love
Float sweet gales of heaven;
And in fullness of pure bliss
Angel joy is given."

He hath words of love and comfort ;
   He hath strength he would impart ;
Let them heal each wounded spirit ;
   Let them sink into each heart :

" Brethren, I am with you always,
   With you to the end of time,
I will bear with you all sorrows,
   Go with you to joys sublime.
Sisters, in this pure relation,
   I would greet you here to-day,
Do not feel that I have left you,
   Do not think me far away.

" I will labor still for Zion,
   Still devoted to the cause,
Help support her glorious standard,
   Help sustain her sacred laws.
Lo, I feel my spirit blessed,
   Lo, I feel that love divine,
Which to me is of more value
   Than the greatest joys of time.

" And I thank my dear companions
   For the love you 've given me.
O, receive my love and blessing,
   Which unmeasured flows to thee.
I am thankful for my calling,
   Thankful for this blessed day.
Now, with joy and pure rejoicing
   I will hasten on my way.''

THE MISSION AND TESTIMONY OF THE SHAKERS OF THE TWENTIETH CENTURY TO THE WORLD.

A LECTURE DELIVERED AT GREENACRE, ELIOT, MAINE, JULY 19, 1904.

It is the mission of the reaper.

Are the fields white for the harvest? Jesus thought they were in His day.

The sharp sickle in the hands of the reaper is to cut souls from the generative life and garner them into the spiritual.

That was the mission of Jesus,—to teach a higher life than the generative to the few who were able to live that higher life. His words were: "All cannot receive the saying. He that can receive it, let him receive it." And His meaning was,—let him subdue that animal nature into which the spirit of evil, an enemy, has sown tares.

"If any man will come after me, let him deny himself and take up his cross and follow me."

"They that are Christ's have crucified the flesh with the affections and lusts."

"It is a hard saying; who can hear it?" said the murmuring ones. But there were those, even in that day, who did receive it, willingly and thankfully, who by daily self-denial subdued every animal passion, made their spirits beautiful and refined, and entered the spirit life purified and redeemed.

The question is almost always propounded: "If all should do this, what would become of the world?"

"Straight is the gate and narrow is the way, and few there be that find it." So the world is safe, as far forth as the cross of Christ is concerned.

The mission and testimony of the Shakers is as much to those living in the marriage relation as to those who have a call to live above it. The trumpet speaks in thunder tones to those who would bring forth an offspring to people the world: "Your vessels are marred in the potter's hands and must be made over by regeneration," were the words of one of the first Shaker Elders.

Every soul that you bring into the world must be born again, from the natural into the spiritual, either in this life or the next.

The Shaker testimony is, to-day, and always has been, burning hot against the unfruitful works of darkness, and here is where the Cross of Christ comes in. When the people of the world become perfect in their generations, even as Noah was perfect in his, what an improvement there will be in the race? What noble and God-like men and women will become developed! The golden age will then dawn when Christ will bring in an everlasting righteousness.

As Buddha said to the people in his day, "Hear the five rules aright." So we would lay before you the Karma of the Christian, "Whatsoever a man soweth, that shall he also reap."

And to you who are ripened for the harvest we would say, "Enter the Path." "For," said Buddha, "There spring the healing streams, quenching all thirst! There bloom the immortal flowers." Forsake the plain of nature and come up into the spiritual where Christ is. "They that are Christ's have crucified the flesh with the affections and lusts." You that would people the world, rise above the unfruitful works of darkness. Take not one unnecessary step to satisfy the cravings of a depraved nature.

The impress of the life you live is stamped upon your features. You carry all your animal desires into the next life. There no language is needed, and your thoughts will be open before thousands of spirits, with whom you will come in contact. You will call upon the rocks and the mountains to fall upon you to cover you from the pure eyes of the redeemed. Even here, our thoughts are plainly seen by both the good and the evil spirits who surround us.

"Are not thousands now beholding
Every action, word and way,
And our very thoughts unfolding
In the blaze of endless day?"

Feticide is murder, and can never be tolerated in the light of the new heavens and the new earth which God is creating. Bring up your children in the nurture and admonition of the Lord, for you will be held accountable for the evils you have planted in them that may grow and develop.

Messengers are now abroad in the world who are inspired by the Christ. Here we find, in our beloved Sister Sarah Jane Farmer, a divinely inspired woman whom we greet in the fullness of the love of the angels of the New Creation of God. A voice comes to us from a teacher and man of God in Russia, Count Leo Tolstoi, condemning all those evils that would destroy the human race. The trumpet gives no uncertain sound.

You send missionaries to the Far East to teach the people there your mistakes, when lo, and behold, there are those in those countries who could teach the people of the United States a better life than is generally lived. The teachings of Jesus and the life he lived are a good and sure test for our lives. As said the poet Whittier:

> " Thou judgest us ; thy purity
>   Doth all our lusts condemn ;
> The love that draws us nearer thee
>   Is hot with wrath to them."

Thus we have given you, in plain words, the Testimony of the Shakers of the twentieth century to the world. It is what they have lived out for more than one hundred and twenty-five years. Thousands of them have, by a daily cross, subdued all selfishness and every evil passion, and entered the next life, bright and beautiful spirits.

Principles that can never be overthrown by the advance of science have long been understood in the Shaker Order.

The Duality of God, Father and Mother, Christ, the Divine Spirit emanating from them, able to reach and inspire every soul made worthy by good works. Jesus, the perfect man, born of noble, human parentage, wholly imbued with the Christ, and the Leader into the higher spiritual life.

Progression after death. The travel of the soul from one degree of grace and glory to another throughout the ages of eternity. All the souls who have ever passed from this life into the world of spirits, must sometime enter this progression and be saved by the cross, by walking in the straight and narrow way.

"There is a path which no fowl knoweth, and which the vulture's eye hath not seen. The lion's whelps have not trodden it, nor the fierce lion passed by it."

There will be a great work for the heavenly angels and purified spirits to do to assist those who are far from God, for all those lost ones must be sought out and drawn by love as soon as they desire to receive help.

When the Christ Spirit becomes enthroned in any soul, then the work of separation will commence in that soul. The good from the evil; the wheat from the tares; the sheep from the goats. To the good the soul will say, "Come and live and grow." To the evil the sentence will be: "Depart from me and be destroyed." No compromise with the evil.

Jesus, inspired by the Christ, said: "I am the resurrection and the life." Therefore, the fact that one is living the high life that Jesus lived, does away with all old forms and ceremonies.

You would like to know how the Shaker Order came into being. I will tell you something of it in a few words:

In the year 1770, Ann Lee, a young woman in Manchester, England, belonged to a society called New Lights, originating from the Quakers. They were very zealous and held noisy meetings, which offended those of the established church.

One Sabbath, all in that little, noisy meeting were arrested and imprisoned, Ann Lee with the others. She was married and had had four children, but they all died in infancy.

While she was in prison, the spirit of Jesus came to her and gave her a mission to give to the world—the same mission and testimony that he delivered so many hundred years before, and the same that we give you to-day.

The society and some others received her testimony. She remained in England about four years after this, when, in the words of one of the first old Shaker hymns:

"The Columbian Eagle,
   Borne by an eastern breeze,
Conveyed this little kingdom
   Across the rolling seas."

A man of wealth, by the name of John Hocknell, believed the testimony of Ann Lee, and was one of a company of eight who came to America with her. They arrived in New York the 6th of August, 1774.

John Hocknell bought land and provided them with a home at Watervliet, near Albany, N. Y. He remained faithful through life and was a great help to the Community both financially and spiritually. Others who believed soon came over, which made quite a little company in the home at Watervliet.

A religious revival was in progress at New Lebanon, about twenty-five miles away. Early in 1780 the subjects of the revival found out about Ann Lee, visited her and her people, received the Testimony and gave all they had to her cause. There was a great stir, and thousands from the country round about believed and became firmly established in the faith.

Ann Lee, inspired by the Christ, taught a full consecration, and a denial of all ungodliness and every worldly lust. From this small beginning societies were formed that are now in existence.

She was called Mother from the first, and she is our Mother to-day, clothed in garments of purity, brighter than the noonday sun.

" O Mother ! bright in thy glory,
    We see thee, 'mid halos of light,
  Crowned in thy victory, bathed in purity,
    Thy robes are eternally white."

Her brother, William Lee, and her adopted son, James Whittaker, were two of the number who came with her from England. They became elders and fathers to the people. With her and others they journeyed through several states of the union, holding meetings and making converts; often followed by persecuting mobs, but always sustained by an over-ruling power; always protected when seemingly there was no chance for life or limb. Their converts numbered thousands, and all this was done in four years' time.

Mother Ann Lee died Sept. 8th, 1784, being forty-eight years of age. A little over a month previous to her death, occurred the death of William Lee, which took place July 22d.

All the believers were now left to the care and spiritual guidance of Father James Whittaker. He received able assistance from Joseph Meacham, who was the leader in the revival at New Lebanon and the first to receive the testimony of Mother Ann in America. We call him Father Joseph. Father James Whittaker died July 20, 1787.

Soon after this, under the administration of Father Joseph Meacham and Mother Lucy Wright, the societies were organized in the different states where the word had been planted. A covenant, or constitution was provided by which the communities have been strongly held and guided to this day.

During the years from 1800 to 1805, a great religious revival was in progress throughout the states of Ohio and Kentucky. At that time Shaker missionaries went there from New Lebanon and established six large Shaker societies. Eighteen Shaker societies, scattered over the United States, moved in harmonious union for many years, and I may say, up to this time. We are less in numbers, but the power of the testimony is the same. Principles are eternal.

Under the benign influence of this Order, thousands were reared from childhood to old age, whose lives were as perfect as could be lived in this world. Men and women, enjoying each others' society as brothers and sisters, loving each other with a pure, unselfish love, as high above the lusts of the flesh as heaven is above the lower regions.

Thus an hundred fold of fathers and mothers, brothers and sisters, houses and lands have been realized in this life, and thousands of spirits have entered the eternal world in clean garments, all selfishness and every evil passion subdued.

We will refer to one phase in the history of the Order. During the year 1837 a spiritual wave rolled through all the Shaker societies—a powerful baptism, similar to that of the Day of Pentecost. The work commenced among the children and passed along, affecting the youth, middle-aged and aged. It continued for years, and was in vogue when modern Spiritualism commenced at Rochester, N. Y., 1848. The work was at its height in all the Shaker societies up to the year 1846, when it subsided in a measure, but has never entirely passed out. The Shakers are now, and always have been, ministered unto by their angel friends, who have passed into the next life.

During the time of this manifestation, from 1837 on through the early forties, books were written by divine inspiration. Thousands of manuscripts were written by the Shaker mediums from those beyond the veil. These are now extant. Many are living at this time, both in and outside the Shaker societies, who were witnesses and can testify to the truth of these things.

Marvelous was the power revealed through the Shaker mediums, who were mostly young brethren and sisters. They were inspired to speak, to write and to sing. Song after song they would sing, new and beautiful, both words and music. These songs are remembered and retained in the archives of the Shaker societies. There were no tipping of tables nor rappings, but the angels spoke to the souls of the people, and were understood.

They were told that the work would go abroad in the world, and were watching for that event to take place, and were not at all surprised at the commencement and subsequent growth of modern Spiritualism.

As it stands to-day the Shakers are well aware of the fraud and deceit practiced by some who claim to stand in the ranks of Spiritualists; but they know it will work itself clear and act as leaven, overthrowing false systems and creeds, and preparing the people for the millennium.

Good and evil are typified by light and darkness. Therefore, if we bring a light into a dark room, the darkness disappears, and inasmuch as a soul is filled with good, evil will disappear.

THEORY AND FACT.

Though all things made must be destroyed,
  Though earthly kingdoms fall,
Forever let us bear in mind
  That heaven is over all.
And when this suffering house of clay
  Is laid beneath the sod,
The thinking spirit shall exist.
  This is decreed of God.
Immortal child, then mourn no more,
But count thy many blessings o'er.

Our earth is surrounded by thousands of elements which our eyes cannot see, finer than the crude air which we breathe, extending beyond the most distant stars throughout the boundless immensity of space. Of these elements our future spiritual homes are composed. Of these elements our spiritual bodies are made.

God, our infinite Mother, created the beautiful things, the flowers and the singing birds, music and the visions which flow into the soul of the poet. She is forever drawing us nearer and nearer unto her beautiful Self, the source of elegance and refinement. She is leading us beside the still waters.

Christ is the overbrooding love emanating from our Heavenly Father and Mother.

Christ is the Crown which the Christian Pilgrim saw the Angel holding over the head of the man who was digging in the dirt with a muck rake, and never raising his eyes from his sordid employment. As he never looked upward, he did not know of the Angel, nor of the Crown, which he might have for his own by paying the price.

Jesus was a perfect man, who gave his whole life to do good. And the Christ spirit descended upon him in the form of a dove and remained with him.

The same beautiful spirit came to his disciples as the Comforter at the Day of Pentecost.

Jesus was a man without fault, inspired by the Christ.

Ann Lee was a woman without fault, inspired by the Christ.

Any one can become the Christ, by subduing every animal passion and rising to a high and pure life.

"They that are Christ's have crucified the flesh with the affections and lusts."

When I say "Christ" I mean the Spirit.

When I say "Jesus" I mean the Man.

Jesus was the Christ when he said, "Come unto me all ye that labor and are heavy laden and I will give you rest," etc.

Jesus was the Man when he overturned the money tables, and drove the people from the temple.

He evidently regretted that rashness which so jarred upon His gentle Spirit, for he was soon heard to repeat the quotation, "The zeal for My Father's house hath eaten me up."

Thousands of young women, ruined by their own and the lust of men, are committing suicide to cover their disgrace. The testimony against that depraved nature should be powerful enough to cause men and women to hate it with a perfect hatred, and to rise so high above it in spirit, as never to entertain one thought of indulgence.

From above the magnificence of the landscape in a beautiful morning, and the sublimity of the rolling waves of the ocean; from above the grandeur of the rising and setting sun, and all the glories that this world can bestow; from above all these, there cometh an inspiration, clothing the purified spirit in garments of beauty, revealing the name of God written upon the forehead of the undefiled soul. Thus shall the Children of Light stand before the multitude.

The Cross of Christ is now to be brought very closely home.

The Shaker Order is founded upon three unchangeable principles:

First.—Upon joining this Society, a confession of every sin that one has ever committed, which can be called to mind, must be made in the presence of a living witness of his or her own sex, one who has gone through the same crucial test.

Second.—From henceforth a life above the order of natural generation is required in letter and in spirit. If one falls from this high standard he ceases to be a Shaker until restored by confession and repentance.

Third.—There must be a community of interests, a settlement with lawful heirs of whatever property one has in possession, and what there is over given to the Society with a consecration of time and labor, for the good of the Cause. This is not accepted by the Society until one has had ample time for consideration. If, after this, he falls away, the Society is under no obligation to return to him all that he thus willingly gave, but in such cases a satisfactory settlement has generally been made.

Comments relating to the preceding:

"I looked, and lo, a Lamb stood upon Mount Zion and with Him an hundred, forty and four thousand," having the name of God written upon their foreheads. These are the undefiled followers of Jesus. They have washed their robes and made them white by living the life that Jesus lived. A new song is in their souls, which only the undefiled can learn, and all the promises to the overcomer are theirs, the white stone with the new name, etc. These have been searched as Jerusalem, with candles.

The time is at hand when God will shake terribly the

earth. Watch and see the creeds fall and the false systems overturned. He will "stain the pride of all flesh and bring into contempt the haughtiness of man." When the conscience of any one brings him to that condition that he is willing to appear before God in judgment, and in the presence of one of his fellowmen who has done the same work himself, make a confession of all his sins, he will find his pride stained and his haughtiness brought into contempt. He will also find that he has become a child of God.

> How plain the outward mien bespeaks the mind,
> And shows the heart that's to the will of God resigned.
> There's love in every action, word and way,
> Which all around can feel from day to day.
> These have risen to the beautiful life of the Christ.
> Their motives all are just, their hearts are pure,
> And nothing base and vile can they endure.
> No selfishness in them can find a place.
> What greater picture can be found of Heavenly Grace!

CHRIST, THE SPIRIT,—JESUS, THE MAN.

I saw a light descending,
　'T was hidden many years.
I saw a spirit bending
　From trans-meridian spheres.
Now brooding o'er the waters,
　That light has taken form,
Which nineteen hundred years ago,
　Spoke peace and calmed the storm.

The spirit form of Jesus,
　The man of God's own choice,
Who held spell-bound the thousands
　And demons feared his voice,
Still reigns in realms of brightness,
　The first begotten Son,
The head of many brethren
　Who unto him have come.

The beautiful Christ spirit
　From earth was far away,
In waiting and in watching,
　Might have been there to-day,
Had not this man of Israel,
　By prayer and faith and love,
Called down this regal Spirit,
　Whose form was like a dove.

This spirit rested on him,
　And claimed him for a son,
'T was then that God's true Order,
　On earth was first begun.

Confucius, Zoroaster
   And Buddha of renown,
Hundreds of years before that time
   Through vistas dark, looked down,

And saw this lovely Messenger,
   On Judea's sacred plain,
When loud, unto the nations,
   This truth did each proclaim,
And prophesied the coming
   Of that eventful day
When Christ should be revealed to man,
   And show the perfect way.

That light again was hidden,
   Although so very bright,
And darkness covered all the land,
   God's work was out of sight.
But now it shines again on earth,
   Most beautiful to see,
A queen is decked in royal robes
   We call her name Ann Lee.

Printed in the United States
1162300001B/191-192